D1091577

RAISING
GOD'S
CHILDREN

Anita Bryant and Bob Green

RAISING
GOD'S
CHILDREN

Fleming H. Revell Company
Old Tappan, New Jersey

Scripture quotations in this volume are from the King James Version of the Bible.

The Ann Landers column is reprinted from the *Sentinel-Star*, Orlando, Florida, by permission of the Field Newspaper Syndicate.

"Hang in There, Anita" is from *Florida Baptist Witness* and is used by permission of Edgar R. Cooper, Editor-Manager, *Florida Baptist Witness*.

Material by Les Ollila is used by permission of Life Action Ministries, Buchanan, Michigan 49107.

Excerpts from Concerned Christian Mothers Fact Sheet are used by permission of Concerned Christian Mothers, Inc., P.O. Box 1702, Carol City Station, Opa Locka, Florida 33055.

Library of Congress Cataloging in Publication Data

Bryant, Anita.
    Raising God's children.

      1. Family—Religious life. 2. Children—Management. 3. Bryant, Anita. 4. Green, Bob. I. Green, Bob, joint author. II. Title.
BV4526.2.B73   248'.84   77-13762
ISBN 0-8007-0878-4

Contents

RAISING
GOD'S
CHILDREN

Bob

1
Raising God's Children

Miss Jackie Lee, my smart and efficient young assistant at Fishers of Men Opportunities, Inc., our Christian talent booking agency, sailed into my office and dumped an armload of letters on the desk.

"We've got a few hundred questions to answer, Bob," she announced energetically, pointing to the stacks of mail. "Funny, but when you read these you're going to find the same questions popping up again and again.

"Why don't you and Anita do yourselves a favor? Why don't you just write a book called *Raising God's Children?*"

I laughed. "You'll never believe this, Jackie," I began, playing it cool, "but Anita and I are discussing that possibility with our publishers right now—and you just came up with the book title!"

Jackie stared at me suspiciously, certain I was putting her on. When she decided it was for real she broke out in a big grin. "Super!" she said. "It's got to be easier to write a book than answer all this mail!"

Anita Bryant, my wife, doesn't agree with that. She has said that each book (this is her seventh Christian book and the fourth in which I've been involved) has been born out of severe growth pains in our own family life.

This one will be no exception. Anita Bryant, since 1968 recognized as the tremendously popular Florida Orange Juice girl, presently finds herself highly controversial—complete with threats, boycotts, a conspiracy to destroy her career, all manner of ridicule and harassment. Meanwhile I, Bob Green, traditionally the behind-the-scenes guy, who sticks to managing our various business enterprises, find myself out front at public meetings, legal hearings, interviews with the media.

This book is written during some of the most trying months of our seventeen-year marriage. Our family life has been tested continuously; often we ask ourselves if it ever again will be the same.

That's what can happen, fellow Christians, when we're called to take a public stand for Jesus Christ. Things can get very rough. But the good news—and every member of our household testifies to this—is that God is faithful. His word is true. He provides the strength, the faith, the peace of mind we need. And through it all, our kids have been fantastic. We all look at this period of trials and tribulations as one of spiritual family growth.

Ironically, the issue which thrust us into the news involves the very premise around which this book is written—that American parents should have the final say-so as to how their children are reared.

Is it possible to raise God's children in man's society? Anita and I are not alone in asking that question. Every day letters arrive from readers in every part of America and even beyond, asking for practical, down-to-earth advice about child rearing.

Your letters convince me that our family's not unique in our conviction that it's time we stop turning our kids' rearing over to the so-called experts, agencies, and institutions—and start working really hard at being parents. God gave us not only the authority, but the responsibility to do just that.

At this point I'd like to introduce you to (or update you on) the Bob Green family. Our household probably compares in many ways to yours: two working parents; four children, including two teenagers and two sub-teens; an assortment of dogs, cats, birds and other creatures and "critters"; a complex of homework, music, and dancing lessons, track meets, household chores and you-name-it; six people of various ages and needs who try to walk the Christian walk, to put Christ at the center of the whole ball game.

We're proud to live and work in Miami Beach. It's no secret that the Greens are great Florida boosters. Anita's position as spokeswoman for the Florida Citrus Commission is something we especially prize, since it rests a great deal on her personal and professional commitment to God, country, and high moral standards. We're proud of the Citrus Commission and the many individual growers we count as our personal friends.

Anita Bryant has been called America's most versatile entertainer; her performing career compares to no other. She was just a teenager when she cut her first gold record, and from there she's enjoyed a steady climb into concerts, summer stock, recording, radio, television, and personal appearances of many sorts.

She has sung for royalty, for presidents, and for American servicemen at military posts all over the globe, as well as forgotten patients in veterans hospitals and obscure nursing homes.

Anita represents some of America's most important civic clubs, industries, and patriotic organizations. She speaks and sings at churches all across America, on the "700 Club" and the "PTL Club," at Billy Graham Crusades, on Oral Roberts' TV specials, Jerry Falwell's "Old Time Gospel Hour" television show, Cecil Todd's Revival Fires and commentates the great Orange Bowl Parade, Junior Orange Bowl Parade and Super Bowl extravaganzas here in Miami.

You can imagine how proud of Anita I feel. But believe me, the most extraordinary fact of her whole career is that she steadily refuses to compromise her Christian testimony. She literally does it all as unto the Lord, and she always has. I know of no other personality who would be willing to put her career on the line as Anita has done.

Anita's top role is that of Christ-follower; she truly is a godly woman. I honor her most of all for that, and for all she means to me as a Christian wife and the mother of our four children.

I thank God for our marriage. He has melded my former career in broadcasting and Anita's career as a performing artist into something really creative and satisfying. Besides heading Bob Green Productions, Inc. and Fishers of Men Opportunities, Inc., I manage Anita's ever-growing career and try to keep it within bounds. It's tough keeping things uncomplicated enough to provide prime time for our home, kids, church activities, and ourselves.

We invest a lot in our children. Bobby, our oldest, is fourteen. He's really a responsible boy, highly dependable and trustworthy, and super talented. The younger kids very much look up to him.

Gloria Lynn is thirteen and becoming a beauty. She's excellent at piano and wins prizes and breaks records at track, and she's a good mixture of little girl and young lady.

Billy and Barbara, our twins, are almost nine. Barbara has begun to play her mommie's records and sing along, copying her style exactly. Billy's still the physical-fitness kid, but now he's into oil painting as well.

One interesting thing we did is interview all four of our kids for this book. Some of their comments turned out to be quite revealing—especially their opinions on discipline.

You see, Anita and I don't claim to be super authorities on child rearing. Ask me or any other father of four, in fact, and we're likely to testify that we become less and less dogmatic on the subject of kids as the years go by.

What's more, as our plans for this book shaped up, more than one person expressed heavy doubts: "Look, Bob, you're not home free yet. Sure as this book comes out, one of your kids could do something wild and get his name in the newspaper. It's happened to some very prominent people, even Christian people. Kids get into every kind of trouble anymore. Aren't you sticking your neck out?"

Sure! I've often said that where people are concerned, there's no model that comes with any kind of guarantee. People—including children, adults, pastors, relatives, bosses, political leaders and all the rest—can fail you at any point.

That's the bad news.

The good news, however, is that God *does* give us parents a guarantee. An absolute, certified blanket statement comes with every child that's ever born. It's foolproof (if we obey it), even for those kids who get involved in the kind of escapade that makes everybody unhappy. God's guarantee shapes up like this:

> Train up a child in the way he should go: and *when he is old,* he will not depart from it. (The italics are mine.)
>
> Proverbs 22:6

It's up to us parents to do the training, according to God's Word. *Raising God's Children* will explore some of our God-given rights and responsibilities as child trainers, in an age when American parents are copping out by the millions. The tragedy of one million divorces a year is enough to destroy any nation.

I believe the job we parents are doing in many respects is becoming a national disgrace. Fathers and mothers are turning to the dictates of the so-called experts. They're looking in all directions for answers to really bizarre influences their children encounter nowadays—even such far-out things as witchcraft, occult, child pornography, group sex, homosexuality, pornographic reading materials, and suggestive and often offensive records.

Think of the number of parents into behavior modification techniques for their subteen children, or hypnosis, or psychiatry. Hundreds of thousands of young Americans classified as "hyperactive" stay perpetually drugged—under doctor's orders, with parental consent and school enforcement.

Meanwhile school counselors inherit the job of coping with children whose minds, bodies, and wills have been weakened by marijuana, speed, and all the rest; high schoolers who need Alcoholics Anonymous; first graders whose mommies and daddies put the kid's name on a psychologist's waiting list as a natural step in their upcoming divorce plans; and girls so young they've never been invited to a prom—but need an abortion clinic.

Does all this sound way-out? Then consider a more "normal" picture of today's child: He watches television an average of thirty-seven hours per week; not fond of exercise and not required to walk or ride a bike to school, he becomes passive and sedentary; he's overweight due to improper diet and lack of exercise; in 50 percent of all cases, both parents work outside the home; due to lack of time, his parents offer him little or no consistent discipline or religious training; and in six out of ten cases, he is a product of divorce.

No wonder American Roman Catholic bishops believe their highest priority for improving religious education is to begin changing the culture of the United States!

A United Press International story recently quoted from a fifty-two-page study forwarded to the Vatican from the United States, in which prelates said, "The

United States has been moving away from at least a semblance of allegiance to and practice of Christian values to the condition of a secularized and even . . . amoral society."

The report described our society as "a culture that has been deteriorating through divorce, abortion, increased crime and juvenile delinquency, drug abuse, alcoholism, sexual abuses and deviations, etc."

Predictably, the study recommended that "the family needs to be supported and strengthened, for all indications are that it is breaking down alarmingly in our society."

Does this indicate that most American parents no longer care about their children? No, I don't believe that for a moment. People *do* care—they care desperately—but so many parents don't know who to believe any more. They've lived to see even Dr. Spock admit some of his theories didn't work. What other authority can they trust?

Anita and I claim the authority of the Holy Bible. Jesus said, "Heaven and earth shall pass away, but my words shall not pass away" (Matthew 24:35). Knowing God placed every rule for healthy human behavior in His Word, we searched there for new insights.

We can't find any place in the Bible where God requires parents to be *experts*—but He does require them to be *parents!*

He tells us to train, exhort, admonish, teach, and discipline our children in love—and that's full-time work. Nowhere does He say we need to be psychologists, or have any super knowledge of human behavior in order to raise our kids, but again and again we're warned that God holds us responsible for what we do or do not teach our children.

That's we parents, personally. Not the school systems, the U.S. Department of Health, Education and Welfare, not society at large, the church, the Boy Scouts or any other group—but the individual father and mother of that individual child. God holds *us* accountable.

A column by Ann Landers contains some thought-provoking ideas for us parents, and bears reprinting here:

DEAR ANN LANDERS: A long time ago you printed Twelve Rules for Raising Delinquent Children. I didn't pay much attention way back then because I had three small children who showed no sign of going wrong. Today, I think I have a couple of hooligans on my hands, and one "possible."

What about a repeat, Ann? Now, as I look back, those rules were probably Landers at her best.

FLAGSTAFF MOTHER

DEAR MOTHER: The Twelve Rules for Raising Delinquent Children were not original with me. They were sent by a reader who credited the Houston (Texas) Police Department. I am pleased to rerun them for you—and for others who may not have seen them the first time around.

1. Begin with infancy to give the child everything he wants. He will then grow up to believe the world owes him a living.

2. When he picks up bad words, laugh. This will make him think he's cute. It will also encourage him to

pick up cuter phrases that will blow off the top of your head later.

3. Never give him any religious training. Wait until he is 21 and then let him decide for himself. (Don't be surprised if he decides to be "nothing.")

4. Avoid the use of the word "wrong." It might develop a guilt complex. This will condition him to believe later, when he is arrested for shoplifting or stealing a car, that society is against him and he is being persecuted.

5. Pick up everything he leaves lying around—his books, shoes and clothing. Do everything for him so he will become experienced in throwing all responsibility on others.

6. Let him read any printed matter he can lay his little hands on. Make sure the silverware and glasses are sterilized but allow his little mind to feast on garbage.

7. Have plenty of knock-down, drag-out fights in the presence of your children. Then, after you are divorced, they will not be surprised.

8. Give the child all the spending money he wants. Never let him earn his own. Why should HE have things as tough as YOU had them?

9. Satisfy his every craving for food, drink and comfort. See to it that every sensual desire is gratified. Childhood should be FUN! Denial may lead to harmful frustration.

10. Take his part against neighbors, playmates, friends, teachers and policemen. They're all prejudiced against your child.

11. When he gets into real trouble apologize for yourself by saying, "I never could do a thing with him."

12. Prepare for a life of grief. You are apt to have it.

Okay, so that's how *not* to raise our children. The good news is, God gives us every "how to" we'll ever need for rearing kids in chaotic times. For example, Ephesians 6:4 in The Amplified Bible says, "Fathers, do not irritate *and* provoke your children to anger—do not exasperate them to resentment—but rear them [tenderly] in the training *and* discipline and the counsel *and* admonition of the Lord."

That says it all. At this point, when everybody's looking for the last word—the leading expert on any given subject—why not go to the Top with our questions on child rearing?

Why not ask God to be our divine Consultant?

And what happens, anyhow, when parents decide to allow God to be their Authority?

As an amateur parent along with all the other amateur parents, I've just one observation to make: I have yet to meet any parent, child or child-development expert *anywhere* who has used God's methods and claimed they don't work.

God's eternal principles still work perfectly—when we utilize them. Despite the evils that threaten to inundate our society, it's still possible to raise God's children. As parents, we need to pray that God will revive every family in America, beginning with the father.

And at the Green's house, that means me.

Anita

2
Lord, Send Revival

The note came from a Christian sister, our friend from church, and her words surprised me. "Let me say the Lord has convicted me of sin concerning you," she wrote. "I have judged you and have had terrible un-Christian thoughts regarding you. Please accept my apology. I want you to know I'm backing you up one hundred percent, and pray the Lord keeps you safe through all this."

She signed her name and added a postscript: "It feels so good to get this off my mind! Praise the Lord for revival!"

Amen! The surge began early in January and quickly gathered into a congregation-wide wave of prayer for God to send us real, old-fashioned revival. Led by our pastor, Brother Bill Chapman, we at Northwest Baptist Church felt a need, a longing, for a fresh touch of God in our lives.

New prayer groups formed. An almost tangible sort of excitement built as we waited on the Lord, expecting Him to burst one of His spiritual bombshells in our midst. And as I prayed, I felt I had to be the hungriest, the neediest of all. I begged God to send revival to our family, our church, our country—and that He would begin it in me.

Well, as Grandma Berry used to say, "Be careful what you pray for; you might get it."

God did answer my prayer—explosively. (Had I dreamed of some of the ways He'd answer, I might never have prayed it.)

Did you ever look around your household and wonder how everybody got so disorganized, fragmented, and discontented? It's amazing how quickly a family of six can run off in different directions—how soon the setup can go to pot.

No wonder I prayed for revival! The kids had begun to bicker a lot. Prayer altar was almost fading out of the picture because we were so busy; worse, it got so hardly anyone even seemed to miss it. Thanks to our schedule we'd almost stopped attending Sunday and Wednesday evening church services. In short, little by little our family's spiritual life was drying up—and it showed!

On the good side of the ledger, Bob and I had completed a super-fantastic year of strenuous business in 1976—literally three times as many bookings as I'd ever had before—and God went before us every step of the way. We really felt grateful to God, yet, as America's unforgettable Bicentennial Year ended, I felt a tremendous letdown.

The familiar anxieties began to build within me. It's the almost inevitable price a working woman pays, with feelings of real inadequacy where her household is concerned. This is my biggest bugaboo, the place where Satan tries to worm his way into my thinking.

So I got very discouraged. *God, what will it profit me if I gain the whole world and lose my household, I asked. How do you want me to serve my husband? Our children? Whatever happened to the sweet spirit we used to feel around here? Why do I feel so resentful? Help!*

I began to spend much more time praying for each individual family member. I asked God to indwell me, and to teach me to minister to my husband and our four strong-minded youngsters. I prayed for revival to sweep through our church, too.

As I prayed, I took stock, and as I surveyed our family life I felt more and more pessimistic. I could see critical attitudes in the children, in Bob and me. We had sacrificed our close fellowship in the church family for a time, mostly because of our heavy travel schedule—and it showed. I felt like I'd been starved to death, and I couldn't take it any longer. It just broke my heart.

I realized my heart had grown cold, and I knew God held me accountable for the spiritual feeding of my children. I committed all this to prayer. *God, I just give up, I really give up. I give up on Bob and the children and the whole ball of wax. Bob keeps forgetting to lead us to the prayer altar, the kids don't care any more, and if I say anything at all I'll explode. You've got to give me the strength and the desire to pick up and start over. I've lost my desire. I'm tired of carrying the whole burden. My own attitude is lousy too, and I can't do anything about it . . . .*

That's where I began, by praying for revival in me. I saw my own sin condition; it was sin against God, and Him alone. I saw the danger of it, and its possible consequences not only in my life but throughout the family. God says if one member suffers, the whole body suffers.

Also, once your spiritual life slumps and you do ask God to speak, you'd better obey immediately. After all, if you don't obey He is going to stop speaking to you in those areas.

One day, the Lord got hold of my heart. I have taught Sunday school for four years, but He told me to commit myself to further work in the church on Sunday evenings, whether or not anybody else in the family came along. I found myself going forward to offer to work with training union. I had to make that commitment publicly.

Then I began to feel peace. Gradually I saw God working in our home, and I knew He was working on me. My personal revival started, even before the fantastic Life Action revival team arrived to set our church spiritually on fire.

Then, would you believe, Bob and I were booked to be out of town during revival! Our family snow/ski vacation at Sun Valley, Idaho—something we'd prayed about and worked toward all year—coincided with revival week at our church. *We desperately need that vacation,* I told God, *but our family needs revival even more. Why does it have to work out this way?* I cried out in protest. *Do something for us!*

He answered in a strange, strange way. What happened at that point will change the course of our lives forever.

But I'm getting ahead of my story. When God intervened He changed all our family plans. We did stay home. Within days our names began to hit every newspaper in the United States. The Green family was forced to cancel our long-awaited vacation retreat, and we began to dig in for a long, hard battle instead.

Meanwhile, God gave us one short, important week in which to prepare each one—even the twins—for a long period of indescribable stress and personal attack. During that week He sent the Life Action revival team to Northwest Baptist, and our church entered into a tremendous time of renewal.

Led by evangelist Del Fehsenfeld, Jr., a dynamic Christian still in his twenties, the team ministered to the church—including each member of our family—in a special way. Even the twins became members of the "Dynamite Club," and they loved it. The older kids set a good example, so all four of our youngsters really committed themselves to Christ in a whole new way. In fact, each of us committed ourselves afresh to the call of the Lord on our lives.

It's important to convey what God did for us, and what revival means. Bob and I feel America is so hungry for the Bread of Life, so thirsty for the Living Water. We know that even dedicated, committed Christians can become terribly dry. We know the wretched feeling of coming out of the stream of the Spirit, of losing fellowship with God little by little, and not even realizing it.

Here's a wonderful description of God's revival process, written by Les Ollila of Life Action's Family Seminar Department. If only every American family could read this excerpt prayerfully! Les wrote:

What is a real revival? When God sends revival at least three things will happen in our lives. We will *wake up* and stop sinning, we will *break up* the fallow ground, and we will *take up* the cross.

Obedience puts feet to willingness. There is no longer just a willingness to do right but a total obedience in doing what God says. Consider the three points mentioned.

We must wake up. The Word of God says "Awake to righteousness, and sin not; for some have not the knowledge of God: I speak this to your shame" (1 Corinthians 15:34). Waking up involves a decision to separate from sin unto holiness. This involves a rearrangement of priorities in the Christian's life. "But seek ye first the kingdom of God and His righteousness; and all these things shall be added unto you" (Matthew 6:33). Christians in so many cases are putting everything ahead of God in their lives. The word *awake* means to "awake as from a drunken stupor"! Often God's people are living in a stupor of unreality and have their heads in the sand like an ostrich, not aware of what is happening around them. A person in a drunken stupor is insensible. He has no feeling. Also he lives in a fictitious world and does not look at things realistically. However, the drunken stupor is not permanent—it wears off. Eventually awakening must come. How many of us need to be awakened and stop sinning. "Be not drunk with wine, wherein is excess, but be filled with the Spirit" (Ephesians 5:18).

Why do we need to wake up? The world is going to Hell around us and we don't seem to care. Those who know not God, need the Gospel's power, seen in the life of the believer. Also

awakening is needed because the rapture of the
Church is near, "And that, knowing the time,
that now it is high time to awake out of sleep: for
now is our salvation nearer than we believed"
(Romans 13:11). The night is far spent and the
day is at hand: let us therefore cast off the works
of darkness and put on the armour of light. When
genuine revival comes, holiness and purity of life
is a natural by-product.

Wake up? God Himself was about to shake Bob and
me awake, The words of young Les Ollila proved to be
prophetic, for unbeknownst to us, our personal awak-
enings already had gotten underway.

Brother Bill Chapman, our strong and godly pastor,
sounded a warning in church one day—a warning I
nearly missed. He called our attention to a proposed
new amendment to local ordinances regarding alleged
discrimination in housing, employment, and public ac-
commodations. The amendment prohibited discrimination due to "sexual preference."

I failed to grasp the implications of it, but Brother Bill
spelled it out; the amendment was designed to give
special privileges to homosexuals, he informed us. He
suggested that some church members might attend the
public hearing to testify against the proposal.

I left church wondering who would propose such
legislation and thinking, *They should put a stop to it.* I
even felt curious enough to ask Bob who would spon-
sor legislation which could promote open homosexuality.

"Don't you know who sponsored it?" he asked.

"Ruth Shack, unfortunately."

"Ruth?" I felt tremendous dismay. Ruth is Dick Shack's wife, and he was my booking agent. Dick had asked me to endorse Ruth during her campaign for a county commissioner's post, and I agreed. We made a healthy monetary donation, and Dick urged me to make radio-spot announcements, without a fee, asking voters to support her. I knew Ruth as a capable and intelligent woman, but now it dawned on me that I had known far too little about her attitudes and beliefs.

Several months before all this had happened, Bob and I thought it was terrific for Ruth to run for a county commissioner's job, but already she was sponsoring something offensive to our Christian principles. It really got to me. God pierced my heart as I realized my own immaturity as a citizen.

"I must talk to her," I told Bob. "Maybe she doesn't realize what she's doing. Pray that God will help me reason with her."

"Sure, we'll pray," Bob said, turning aside to let a couple of church ladies speak to me.

"Anita, I voted for Ruth Shack because you endorsed her," one of them told me. "Now what can we do?"

Her question jolted me. What *could* we do? I'd never been politically oriented, nor really well informed about local or national issues. I was not a newspaper reader, and like many another Christian, aside from paying taxes and making sincere efforts to vote properly, I made little other effort to have an effect on government.

That began my awakening process. From that day

forward, I knew I'd make every effort to become informed and stay current with the important issues of our day. The first thing I did was phone Ruth Shack and attempt to understand her position.

Her words dismayed me. She believed the amendment to be necessary to the advancement of civil rights for homosexuals.

"But what about *my* civil rights?" I asked. "Flaunting homosexual teaching in private and religious schools violates my religious beliefs. I believe I have a constitutional right to protect my children from knowledge of practices God calls an abomination."

I offered Scripture passages from Old and New Testaments which backed up my convictions, but they apparently made no impact. She said she considered homosexuals to be a minority group who were enduring discrimination; she had pledged to work toward better job, housing, and other conditions for them.

"But homosexual practices violate not only God's law but the Florida state laws and our local ordinances," I protested. Then I realized the new amendment effectually would supersede all those laws, so I dropped that argument. I made one last attempt: "Ruth, you know we don't hate homosexuals. I'm not interested in seeing them punished.

"On the other hand, I don't want to be compelled by law to hire such a person as my secretary, or rent property to them, or have them teach my children. As a Christian mother I work hard to see that my children are taught wisely and filled with the knowledge of God.

"What if one of *your* daughters, influenced by a schoolteacher, were to become a lesbian?"

"I hope I'd understand," she said gently and firmly. "That's another form of love, you know."

Our positions were poles apart. I felt overwhelmed by sadness and dismay, realizing that if the Word of God didn't speak to someone, no argument I could offer would change that person's heart. I wondered if Ruth thought I hated her as I told her, with a heavy spirit, that I'd have to issue a public repudiation of the endorsement I'd once given her.

It's hard to breach a friendship. There's no joy in taking a public stand against the position of someone you once upheld. I sought the Lord in real agony of spirit, but I knew I'd have to speak out immediately— that there was no other way.

I can't describe the turmoil I felt as I realized the potential ramifications of the decision I knew I must make. As Bob and I wrestled with the issue of whether or not we should publicly protest the legalizing of homosexuality, the Lord began to show us the issue was much bigger than just Dade County, Florida.

Also, we had to consider the career aspect. My non-controversial Christian image was about to get smashed to smithereens. As Bob said, "There goes ten years of goodwill." You shudder to think how your professional reputation might suffer; therefore, common sense says, *Cool it, let the issue go; don't get involved.*

On the other hand, what about the kids? As parents, how could we *not* fight to keep them within a Christian educational framework? Even more importantly, what sort of example would we set them as Christian adults?

Hadn't Bob and I taught them that Christians must be prepared to fight—to the death, if necessary—to uphold God's laws?

I talked to myself a little, argued some, wrestled with my thoughts, and prayed without ceasing. Those hours felt terribly lonely, because even Bob couldn't make my decision for me. That decision was not easy, but it became very, very clear.

I decided to write a personal letter to the nine metro county commissioners, and Brother Bill agreed to help me find the Scripture references I needed. However, he got tied up with hospital calls, so I spent several hours searching the Scriptures on my own. Bob promised to help me compose the letter, but he was on jury duty and then caught a viral infection and wasn't up to it. Meanwhile, I felt increasingly impressed of the Lord to send the letter immediately, since the public hearing was just a week off.

After preparing dinner, tucking the children in bed and taking a long-distance telephone interview, I proceeded to tackle the letter. *Lord, please zap it to me right away*, I prayed. *I'm so tired.* The Lord helped me, but by no means would He let me off the hook entirely: I had to work on that letter until three A.M., a lesson I'll not soon forget.

Hours later I showed my work to our close friend and attorney, Charlie Morgan, Jr., for his opinion. Then Debbie Sullivan, Bob's secretary, and Julie Parker, my secretary, spent the rest of the day typing and hand delivering the nine letters.

Bob thought the Lord helped me write a strong letter, and suggested I read it on a local Christian radio station, which had asked me to appear. Shortly afterwards, someone from our church suggested the same idea, and Peggy Chapman, Brother Bill's wife, agreed to go with me to the station to appear on the "Ted Place Show."

As Peggy and I drove to the radio station, I comforted myself with the thought that I was not fighting Ruth Shack, but her proposed legislation. Then God sent a Scripture to my mind:

> Put on the whole armour of God, that ye may be able to stand against the wiles of the devil.
>
> For we wrestle not against flesh and blood, but against principalities, against powers, against the rulers of the darkness of this world, against spiritual wickedness in high places.

Those words are among my favorites—that entire passage in Ephesians 6:11–20. If you read that glorious passage now, you can imagine how it spoke to me in those circumstances. And in verse 17, He told me to take "the sword of the Spirit, which is the word of God."

Father, of myself I can do nothing. Take me into your Word and show me the truth. Tell me what to do. Tell me how to do it. God, you know I'm not trained in public speaking. I'm not able to argue against highly educated people, and half the time Brother Bill even has to show me how to find the Scriptures I need . . . .

Oh, God! Thank You! Your Word provides every answer for my life, and You just reminded me of my forever-favorite text: "I can do all things through Christ which strengtheneth me." (Philippians 4:13).

I can do *all things* through Christ. For years I have

quoted that Scripture, scrawled it in my books beneath my autograph, repeated it to my children.

Now God Himself quickened those words anew in my heart and mind. I felt filled with peace and joy. I did not see *how* I could do what I knew I must do, but God does not lie. If He said I could do anything in the world I have to through Christ, who is my strength, then that has to be so.

Hallelujah! Revival had come, the revival I prayed for, right there in my powder-blue car. When you pray as you drive, and the very presence of God fills the car: it becomes a temple, an altar; it becomes holy ground.

The light changed. I moved into traffic, headed into who-knows-what, my familiar red leather-bound Bible on the seat beside me.

I need no other road map, I thought. *I need no other directions. In truth, I can do all things through Christ, which strengtheneth me.*

Praise the Lord!

Anita

3

Courage for This Day

At this moment in my life I'd like to scream out to all mothers—*Wake up!* Quit being so selfishly concerned with *"my"* individual concerns, *"my"* projects, *"my"* rights!

We American women are reaching for the golden ring, hoping to establish Utopia for ourselves, and it's a farce—a national farce. While we fight for our individual rights we're allowing our children to be destroyed.

It's hard to be a godly mother these days. It's growing harder and harder to swim upstream against swift, deadly currents of selfishness and immorality.

The Bible warns us of this day. In 2 Timothy 3:1–5 the apostle Paul writes to Timothy:

> This know also, that in the last days perilous times shall come.
>
> For men shall be lovers of their own selves, covetous, boasters, proud, blasphemers, disobedient to parents, unthankful, unholy,

Without natural affection, truce-breakers, false accusers, incontinent, fierce, despisers of those that are good,

Traitors, heady, highminded, lovers of pleasures more than lovers of God;

Having a form of godliness, but denying the power thereof: from such turn away.

Horrifying numbers of parents apparently are "without natural affection": chid battering in the United States, for example, accounted for some five million *reported* cases last year. We're also seeing increased numbers of child murders, molestation, exploitation of children for pornographic purposes, and child neglect that cuts across every strata of society.

Even some of America's smartest, best educated, most gifted women are so concerned with *I-I-I* that they devote themselves to their own higher education while they leave their kids' primary education pretty much to others. Meanwhile, as they fight for women's rights, who fights for children's rights? Who will keep our children from being devoured by evil forces we're too busy to recognize?

Survey the women's magazines if you'd like some ideas of what editors and publishers believe American mothers to be preoccupied with. You'll find sex surveys; reports on extramarital affairs with statistics on who participates and how often; and the less than edifying information that today's wife and mother feels almost as free to be unfaithful as does her husband. Of course, such articles don't just discuss unfaithfulness, but also the ability of husband or wife to "handle" the accompanying guilt.

No, you don't read much inspirational stuff in the women's magazines beamed to America's young mothers—unless you count the sumptuous food and decorating pages. You're more apt to find articles encouraging women to do their own thing; gear up for jobs outside the home; protect their credit so they'll be in good shape in case of divorce; and even the legal and "etiquette" problems of living with or traveling with someone not your husband, and similar garbage.

Meanwhile, back in the families God instituted, He hasn't changed the rules on us. He still holds a husband accountable for his household, even if that husband abandons his family: God holds him responsible, and the man someday will answer to the Lord for how he handled *his God-given responsibility.*

But we women will be held accountable by God for our children—their training, their nurture, their cherishing. If God had created me to be a sea turtle I could hatch my eggs and swim away forever. But He didn't. Someday I must answer to Him for *what I did or did not teach my children.*

When you read Second Timothy you see God didn't speak of the father being primarily responsible for the spiritual training of his children. Even the apostle Paul, who called Timothy his "dearly beloved son," said it gave him joy to remember ". , . the unfeigned faith that is in thee, which dwelt first in thy grandmother Lois, and thy mother Eunice; and I am persuaded that in thee also" (2 Timothy 1:5).

God talks about Timothy's grandmother and mother, and about spiritual training being handed down *by women* through the generations. And of course, when God sent a Saviour to the world, He came by means of a woman. So it is primarily through us women that salvation can come for our children, speaking not only physically but spiritually. God planned it that way.

That's the crux of what I want this book to say. The devil is walking around like a lion, ready to devour our children, even as he tempts their mothers to take their eyes off the protection of their children and place them instead on the idols of personal liberation, self-indulgence, so-called "human rights," or "do your own thing."

Also, as society becomes more lax and ultra liberal it's incredible what we allow to come into our homes—even into Christian homes. We're totally used to profanity and even blasphemy on television, pornography in books and magazines, even smutty entertainment ads on billboards and in family newspapers. Many people have gotten so far away from the Word of God that they don't know what's right any more.

That's especially true of the mother—because she's concerned with finding the answer to her problems; or she claims her husband is this, or he's that; he discriminates against her, or puts her down; she's not fulfilled, she's not satisfied . . . and on and on.

If women are allowing their children to go to the dogs, however, they seem to be failing their husbands even more. Indeed, most women attend to their children's needs before they'd even attempt to serve their mate—which is the *man's* fault. Few men today make much serious effort toward following God's plan for establishing a household.

Viewed from man's perspective, it's a gloomy picture. The facts, the statistics, get worse each year. Many
young couples choose not to bring children into our
dirty, polluted, crime-riddled world—they actually fear
to try to raise children!

Viewed from God's perspective, however, the Christian sees a different view—that of man's sins and fail-
ures always overlaid with the blood of Jesus. ("And
almost all things are by the law purged with blood; and
without shedding of blood is no remission" [Hebrews
9:22].) God's promises to His people present shining
hope to any age, no matter how degenerate. As Paul
wrote in Second Timothy 1:7, "For God hath not given
us the spirit of fear; but of power, and of love, and of a
sound mind." And as he wrote in verse 12, ". . . I
know whom I have believed, and am persuaded that he
is able to keep that which I have committed unto him
against that day."

Hallelujah! The Christian can view everything from
the perspective of the Cross. But it sobers us, it's un-
bearable, to realize how many Americans are blinded
to the truth because they don't know the *real* truth,
which is God's Word.

They have gotten away from it and watered it down.
The pleasures of this world have become far more im-
portant than reading God's Word and doing God's will.
It's heartbreaking.

On the other hand, there's a strong network of God's
people praying for a revival in America. And I believe
God wants us to make that choice, just as He wants us
to choose the way we raise our children and choose
how we live out our lives before others. He wants us to

choose His way out of our own free will, in love. I believe He is giving this nation an opportunity, and I don't believe it's too late.

For many years I have prayed for God to bless America. Even during my shows when I sing "God Bless America" I sing it as a prayer, that He'll bless America and bring her a revival. That's been the heart cry of our church and of many, many Christians everywhere who have this burden.

So God says, "Okay, you have the burden now and you have the opportunity to serve Me. I am waking you up to what's happening. You have a space of time in which to do something about it, and if you don't the door will be closed."

I believe God has heard the fervent prayers of His righteous people in America—and if God doesn't answer prayers, He's not on the throne.

I know God wants us to repent, and turn from our wicked ways, and live—and I feel sure the time is short. That's why I'm willing to go and give everything, or do anything, that God wants.

The length of a generation is so short. We have only so much time in which to train our children and teach them the Lord's ways before we see *them* training *their* children, and then we see our children's children. And the evil we allow, we'll see perpetuated.

Doctor Bob Gray, pastor of Trinity Baptist Church of Jacksonville, Florida, and founder and president of Trinity Baptist College, preached a sermon in our church recently that brought my heart into my throat. He said we Christians get so hung up on God's grace and love that we don't talk about repentance, being responsible to God, doing His will, and showing the fruits of the Spirit.

He described how someday we'll stand before Christ's judgment seat and be judged for how we chose to live: he drew a graphic word picture of that time.

Doctor Gray said we'd experience pain, suffering and loss as we were judged by Jesus and saw our own lives through His eyes. And then he offered this vivid scene:

> It's as though you woke up in the night with your house burning. The wife is lying with her husband, but there's no time to wake your husband, no time to grab purse or jewelry, nor get to your children or the pet dog. There's just a little space of air; all you can do is get down, crawl through, and get out. Then you stand outside and watch your loved ones burn. You watch everything that is precious to you burn up. Your house and all your life's work burns to the ground.

Then Dr. Gray said, "Are you going to nudge your neighbor and say, 'Whee! I got out by the skin of my teeth!'?"

No, you will suffer agonizing loss. You will realize untold sorrow and depths of despair in that you did not tell your husband about Jesus, that you did not lead your children to Christ. You weren't the example you should have been; your life was wasted; and as you contemplate your safety, you also realize the horror of your family's lostness.

Brother Gray described how we would experience that overwhelming sense of failure and loss, our lack of faithfulness, even as we looked into the face of Jesus—even as His eyes searched our hearts and souls, seeing we have nothing, nothing whatever to give Him.

This description made me imagine the weeping and wailing, the tremendous suffering and loss, as He holds us accountable and responsible for our lives. It really made me realize the responsibility.

Evil is nothing new. The apostle Paul lived in a world tremendously hostile to the Gospel, and told Timothy

> ". . . what persecutions I endured: but out of them all the Lord delivered me. Yea, and all that will live godly in Christ Jesus shall suffer persecution. But evil men and seducers shall wax worse and worse, deceiving and being deceived.
> 2 Timothy 3:11–13

Then comes the passage that makes my heart shout *Amen!*

> But continue thou in the things which thou hast learned and hast been assured of, knowing of whom thou has learned them;
> And that from a child thou hast known the holy scriptures, which are able to make thee wise unto salvation through faith which is in Christ Jesus.
> All scripture is given by inspiration of God, and is profitable for doctrine, for reproof, for correction, for instruction in righteousness:
> That the man of God may be perfect, throughly furnished unto all good works.
> 2 Timothy 3:14–17

Despite the words I just wrote, however, and despite Paul's challenge to "withstand in the evil day, and having done all, to stand," my heart almost stopped at the thought of something God was telling me to do. I had publicly repudiated my allegiance to Ruth Shack and the legislation she had sponsored. Now, it seemed, her amendment would be brought up for a public hearing where interested citizens might testify, and Brother Bill wanted me to appear. So did Bob.

I prayed fervently. My emotions churned for days as I wrestled with that decision, and I couldn't eat or sleep. Worse, Bob seemed to vacillate. One moment, speaking as my business manager, he'd point out how bad it would be for my career—how potentially embarrassing to sponsors, and so forth. The next moment he'd speak as a Christian husband and tell me he couldn't see how I could do less than testify.

So I stayed in a turmoil, and the children knew it. They knew I felt a gut-level fear of the situation, because I couldn't hide that fear. I felt my own inadequacy about entering a courtroom for the first time in my life, being confronted by others who were really learned on points of law and civil affairs. I dreaded it and feared it, but the more I prayed the more it seemed the Lord said, "Go."

The Friday night before that dreaded Tuesday morning hearing, I appeared on the "Ted Place" Show, a local Christian radio show, and was asked to return the next day. I hated to go alone, but Bob had been fighting a flu bug all week, and Gloria had been sent home from school sick the day before. Bob offered to stay home and cook supper for the kids and get them to bed, since I also was scheduled to appear on another local radio program that same night. That was a real act of submission for Bob!

Everybody seemed to have something to do that night—everyone but Barbara. "I'll go with you, Mommie," she chirped, and I sure was glad.

Barbara always wants to go with me, always is interested in what I want or need to do. She plays my records in her room all the time, is very obedient to me, and often I'm very surprised at the profound things about the Lord that come from Barbara's mouth. Billy, her twin, is much the same way. The twins love to express affection, always support me when I'm hassled, and are quick to go to the prayer altar when something needs prayer.

I paid a lot of attention to the road that afternoon, because it was raining. On our way to the radio station, despite my care, a car shot across the road and nearly sideswiped me. That shook me up, so I drove even more cautiously on the wet streets.

At the radio station, the interview and the phoned-in questions really gave me a spiritual boost. They played one of my songs on the show—"Victory in Jesus." Then the Lord provided words for me to speak, and the whole thing ended up being quite edifying.

After the show, Barbara and I climbed into my blue car and headed home to Villa Verde, our strenuous day nearly over. My thoughts clambered all over one another as I maneuvered through heavy traffic, concentrating on the rainy street, pondering the so-called "civil rights" amendment, halfway listening to Barbara's chatter.

Then it happened—a crazy, grotesque three-car collision immediately ahead of me. The screeching brakes, blaring horns; the car ramming a pole, spinning around, ramming a second car; the horrible sound of metal tearing against metal; the look of sheer, helpless terror on the woman's face; it all happened within inches of my car—with no room for me to swerve.

But I did. Don't ask me how, but I did. We turned the wheel, God's angel and I, perfectly—and we missed a terrible, terrible collision literally by two or three inches. I insist that God saved me: I cannot drive *that* well.

And then I withered. I managed to steer the car to the side of the road, and I stopped. My body trembled uncontrollably as I took Barbara's hand and said, "Let's thank Jesus right now for saving our lives."

Barbara just put her little hand in mine and looked into my face with the wisest, most compassionate expression in her eyes. I perceived that she saw my fear, that she understood what I'd been going through in recent days. There had been some times when I felt so scared I couldn't move, that I just got paralyzed—but I know that God does not give us the spirit of fear.

So Barbara took my hand and said, "Mommie, if God can help us in a bad accident like that, can't He help you in the courtroom?"

When she said that I looked at her and nearly started to bawl.

"He can, baby," I said.

Instantly the truth hit me—straight from the mouth

of a babe. I realized God's nearness, and that I need not fear. Nothing would touch me or harm my family unless God allowed it for His purpose. If God could guide me out of one danger, He could guide me through all danger—and He would not allow a hair on my head to be touched.

The moment that truth came out of Barbara, I felt the presence of God. I was in real awe, and all I could say was, "Thank You, Jesus. Thank You, Jesus."

Alone with Bob, I described how God had delivered Barbara and me. "It was a terrible three-car collision, but it should have been a four-car collision," I told him.

"And Bob, I know what I'm going to do," I continued. "If God wants me to speak at the hearing, I'll do it."

He didn't say anything immediately. His face had gotten white and he didn't hide the fact he was shook, as I described our near-accident. There's no way I can explain how protective Bob is of the children and me, and the dismay on his face said he wished he'd been driving instead of home in bed.

Looking at him, appreciating his strength, I knew he'd support my decision even if it seemed to fly in the face of all common sense. And another thing—I knew Bob would uphold and comfort me with prayer, even if there should turn out to be bad repercussions.

But he didn't say it with words. Not then. He just put his arms around me and held me.

Bob

4

Love and Discipline

As a father, I've got really strong beliefs about the value of discipline. It goes hand in hand with love: I don't believe you can separate one from the other. Hebrews 12:6, 7 says, "For whom the Lord loveth he chasteneth, and scourgeth every son whom he receiveth.

"If ye endure chastening, God dealeth with you as with sons; for what son is he whom the father chasteneth not?"

We try to run the Green household by Bible precepts. We try to accept each individual for what he or she really is, try to love them all with no strings attached; and we really try to use God's ideas about discipline.

Now, most people use the word *discipline* to mean punish: They say, "I'm going to discipline you," when they really mean, "We're going to take a trip to the woodshed." That's not quite what I mean. A primary meaning of the word, according to Webster, is: "Training that is expected to produce a specified character or pattern of behavior, especially that which is expected to produce moral or mental improvement."

But the proof of the pudding is not what I mean, but what my kids think I mean. Over the years I've learned to get more and more specific, to really spell out the boundaries. I don't say, "Don't touch that." Instead I point to everything about the article they might be tempted to pick up or examine, and list every part of the thing they're required not to touch.

The reason is, kids are smarter than Philadelphia lawyers. They're constantly looking for loopholes. So I try to save us all some trouble.

Seriously, though, you do have to know what's coming through to your kids, when you're trying to train them. You know what you're saying, but sometimes what they think you're saying is something else again. It's all a question of communication—and communication takes time and patience. And repetition—and standing pat and being consistent with them, no matter how hard they try to hoodwink you.

Anita and I try hard to achieve consistency. If they do something that merits a reward, we reward them promptly. If they work hard to earn a paddling, we take time to paddle them right away. It's not convenient always, but on the other hand it's never convenient to produce a rotten, unhappy kid who makes others around him miserable.

For the purposes of writing this chapter, I decided to interview each of the kids to see how they felt about the love and discipline in our home. It seemed like a good idea to take them individually (instead of a group)—and then it occurred to me they might be more diplomatic with me than they would be with an outsider.

I asked a grown-up they know to interview them separately, and to tell them their answers were important—that they'd be used in this book, and that they were to be very frank.

When Anita and I played the tapes, every one said something that in some way surprised us. The most interesting thing we learned, however, is that each of the kids claims to appreciate the discipline he receives. Bobby, our oldest, made a strong case, in fact, for us to raise our expectations of him!

I've decided to quote from Billy's tape, just to give a nine-year-old's views on the value of love, discipline, and the Christian life. We didn't edit a word of it.

Q   Billy, would you rather live in a Christian home or another kind of home?

A   I'd rather grow up in a Christian home because I get to grow up with better examples, to live a better life.

Q   Do you ever pray?

A   I pray every day.

Q   And does Jesus ever help you?

A   Jesus helps me all the time. He helps me do my best in school and everything. He helps me when I run a race, because I just say, "Lord, help me with my running."

Q   Do you think you have too many rules in your house?

A   Houses that don't have some rules have lots of troubles, so you have to end up setting some rules in it.

Q   Do you think it's hard to obey the rules?

A   Rules are simple—if you obey them.

Q   That's a smart answer, Billy. Where did you learn that?

A I learned that from good experience and from church too.

Q Do you think you're a happy person?

A Yep! I sure am!

Q Do you ever tell your friends about Jesus?

A I have friends at my school who don't know Jesus who say all those cuss words. They just do those things and the grown people let them do those things because they aren't saved. They just let them get by with it because almost every kid does it.

Q How does that make you feel?

A I felt sort of ashamed. Sometimes Christians even say them by mistake, when they get really mad, you know, they just do it like once in a lifetime. It's really sad, but that's much better than the kids who aren't saved do.

Q Does Barbara believe what you do?

A Well, I never tested her, but she believes. Barbara and I don't talk about stuff much, but we play together. But we talk about stuff in church and all.

Q What are the best things your mother and father ever taught you?

A About being a good example and showing a witness to other people.

Q Do they set good examples?

A Yep, they sure do. Oh, they're really good Christians, and when they pray they really fellowship with the Lord. I don't know how to pray like they pray! They're really good pray-ers.

Q But you pray well for a nine-year-old . . . .

A Yeah, but I can't pray as good as a preacher.

Q Do you like to go to church?

A Yes.

Q I think you must love the Lord.

A I do!

Q Does Bobby help you when you need to know more about things? Does he try to answer your questions?

A Bobby sets me a good example, but he asks too hard questions, like, "What are all the books of the Bible?" I don't even know all the books of the Bible. I'm just a kid.

Q Does Bobby?

A Yes. He's fourteen, and my big sister is thirteen, and I'm two hours older than my little sister. I'm glad I'm older. I wouldn't want to get stuck with her.

Q What's the best thing about being a Christian?

A You get eternal life!

Q Do you ever fight with your brothers and sisters?

A Yep, I sure do, because other kids do. Most of the time you get into a little discussion and they say, No I didn't and I say, Yes you did, and then you get in a fight and all that stuff. Afterwards I tell my dad and tell him to beat 'em good.

Q Do you ever ask the other one to forgive you?

A Sometimes I do. Usually I just say, Get out of here!

Q Do you think your brother and sisters love each other?

A Yeah, when they're nice they do. Oh, they love me, you know—they're just a normal family.

Just a normal family, okay, that's us. But ordinary as Billy's little ideas might sound, we're learning that they're no longer the generally accepted view of life that most Americans hold. Anita and I played each of these little interviews several times, because it felt good to hear our children say they feel loved and they appreciate Jesus and the church and the whole thing.

But maybe parents don't drive these points home often enough. Maybe we're drilling rules into our children more than we're making sure they feel adequate as individuals; and maybe we're busy being pals with them and taking them on fishing trips, when they're really wishing we'd crack down and be fathers—make them shape up and fly right.

One parental attitude that blows my mind says something like this: "I'm going to let my little three-year-old decide this, that, or the other, because I want her to learn to make her own decision."

Baloney! That comes up a lot these days in the discussions concerning homosexuality—that parents would rather their children make that decision for themselves.

Our home definitely is not run like a democracy, and I can't find any place in the Bible where God says it should be. God says we, as parents, should know what truths are fed to our children's minds, just as surely as we wouldn't serve them garbage on a plate at the dinner table.

My children do not have a large number of choices available to them as regards their upbringing. We permit them to see very few television programs, for example, and even those are strictly monitored. Sure, this makes the kids unhappy—but so be it. Until television cleans up, most shows are strictly off limits in our house.

There's a public-service commercial that says, "It's

ten o'clock. Do you know where your children are?"
That's a good question. Definitely we should know
where they are physically: definitely it's our responsibility to know that.

But look at that question another way. Do we *really*
know where our children are *with the Lord?* Are our
sons and daughters saved? Have we introduced them to
the Word of God?

Do we use His Word as our final authority?

Can I remember when I taught my kids to pray?
When was the last time I prayed with my children individually?

Does that child know that I pray for him? Does he
realize I discipline him because I love him, and I'll always love him enough to chasten him?

But more importantly, is our own witness to our kids
something consistent from day-to-day, year-to-year?
Oh, we blow it at times: we might backslide for a season, but do our kids see us as not just talking the talk,
but also walking the walk?

These are serious questions. I can't answer them in
my own heart as well as I wish I could. But I do know
the Lord holds me responsible for the outcome of all
these things. I know He expects me to instruct my children in His way, live a good life before them, and never
let up.

On God's eternal clock, it's getting very late. Do you
know where your children are?

Anita

5

Your Family's Emotions

Doctor William C. Menninger, the world-famous psychiatrist from Topeka, Kansas, believes every person ought to give his emotions—and his life—a periodic checkup.

He asks: "Do you know whether you are going in the right direction, and most of all where you want to go? Not just in your business alone, but in the important areas: the atmosphere in your home, your relations with the members of your family, your own feeling of status and worthwhileness in life, your own dignity and your own integrity."

Many of us who believe in faithful physical maintenance—medical and dental checkups, inoculations, careful diet, and exercise regimes—the whole bit—have no idea of how to check up on our family's emotional health. I know I didn't, until I experienced a near-emotional breakdown resulting in a profound healing three years ago.

I told a little about that experience in *Light My Candle.* At first I felt reluctant to do so, because I considered my emotional battles to be a negative testimony: I felt ashamed of my condition, ashamed that I had "failed Jesus."

(It's interesting how militant homosexuals have fed that information to the press, thinking readers will think negatively of me. Those individuals can't come to grips with books like ours, and those of other Christians who are not ashamed to confess known sins and share the most personal problems with like believers. We Christians don't have to cower, scheme, or lie to cover up the truth about our lives: consequently, we can know a "peace that passeth all understanding.")

I wrote at that time:

> Now for a dogmatic Christian like me, the idea of emotional disturbance, illness, even temporary imbalance, was something I considered sin. I attributed any kind of emotional problem to a faulty prayer life, being out of God's will, or such.
>
> I still say God not only is the Great Physician, but the Divine Psychiatrist as well. The Christian life leads to health and stable living. Most of us can attest to that from our experience with Christ.
>
> From *Light My Candle*

Amen! The letters that flooded in in response to that book convinced me that many other Christians shared my problems. Because they knew they needed inner healing, they also knew their child rearing needed help. As one young mother wrote, "I want to punish my toddler in love, not from my own frustrations. What can I do about my emotions? How can I trust myself to deal with him correctly?"

That's one of today's most important questions, and there are no pat answers. Haven't most of us parents been inconsistent because we deal with our children according to our feelings? Sometimes we're too strict, sometimes too lenient, and the kids learn to read mommie's moods and stay at arm's length when she's depressed or even hostile.

Three years ago my emotional crisis led Bob to take me to the famous psychological clinic in California run by Dr. Clyde Narramore, the noted Christian doctor, author, and lecturer. My stay was expected to take three weeks, so it's amazing that in just *three days* with the help of the Lord and Scripture, a skillful Christian counselor enabled me to begin to understand and accept myself for the first time in my deep emotions.

It was a really fascinating and painful process, but I thank God for it! That experience developed a new awareness and sensitivity in me regarding other people's and my children's emotional development. As I became stronger in my own personality, I saw the family strengthen; consequently, I urge any parent with known emotional problems to seek expert Christian counseling and ask God to lead you into total healing of mind, body, and spirit. That is God's perfect will for you. As it says in Third John 2, "Beloved, I wish above all things that thou mayest prosper and be in health, even as thy soul prospereth."

During these past five months our family has been subjected to incredible physical, mental, and emotional stress, including such extraordinary occurrences as rioting, picketing, and threats of bombing our home and other types of physical harm to me, my family, and others working for the organization opposed to the amendment.

The children know I have been threatened with assassination, they also know how it feels to have policemen and specially trained dogs search our house for hidden explosives, and they have seen me leave home escorted by bodyguards. Later in the campaign they saw armed guards in front of our home each night.

But praise God, there has been almost no emotional fallout from the bizarre events. If anything, our family has experienced supernatural peace. It's evident to Bob and me that our children understand that the Christian does not have to yield to harassment or fear, but plants his feet on the solid rock of Jesus.

Three years ago I couldn't have exhibited such amazing emotional or physical stamina. Today, by the power of God, Bob and I claim our family unit not only has not suffered lasting damage, but actually is closer, firmer and stronger than ever before.

Understand, we must give God all the credit. Things did not just fall into place, after all. Indeed, during the first weeks of our spiritual warfare Bob and I easily could have been capsized by Satan.

You remember I described our family as being spiritually dry. It was while we were that way, and I was praying for revival, that God jarred our lives further by exploding the homosexual issue in our midst.

Bob and I, tired as we were, found ourselves caught off-balance by the fast-moving events. We had to make independent decisions simply because of time factors, and we don't like to do that. I'd find myself granting press interviews or dealing with sponsors without having time to first discuss things with Bob, and then there'd be no time to brief Bob about what was going on.

He was having to do pretty much the same thing. Satan was up to his divide-and-conquer strategy, and we both knew it. For several weeks the left hand did not know what the right hand was doing. Bob and I both knew we had been catapulted onto a collision course, both of us were experiencing increasing anxiety, but we couldn't seem to change things.

Worse, circumstances produced very bad communication between Bob and me just when we needed it more than at any other time in our lives. I felt God had tapped me on the shoulder and given me direct marching orders. Bob, who knows my nature very well, didn't know whether I had orders from God or was reacting impulsively. Bob's nature is cautious and logical. He is very decisive and strong, but he arrives at his decisions by process—never by impulse.

Bob backed me all the way, but I didn't realize that. The courtroom hearing concerning Ruth Shack's controversial amendment became a disastrous fiasco for the Christians and other moral leaders who attended it; our cause lost. That turned out to be one of the most decisive mornings of my life, because two things happened at that point:

• A homosexual community leader informed the Miami metro commissioners and everyone in the courtroom hearing that even if the so-called "civil rights" amendment were defeated in Miami, it wouldn't

matter—that passage of ERA and other national legislation would get them what they wanted anyhow.
- And the moral leaders of Miami, including Bob Brake
(an attorney and former metro commissioner who
appeared to speak against the amendment in the
courtroom that morning, and whom I never had met
prior to the hearing) asked me to head the cause.
After conferring with Bob, I committed myself to the
task. It seemed we'd have to get at least ten thousand
names signed to petitions if we wanted to request a
local referendum, and we decided to go after those
names. We'd put this issue to a popular vote. So I
pledged myself to the task of helping to galvanize the
spiritual and civic leaders and rallying them to our
cause. Later, Bob Green was to labor in prayer for one
solid day as the Lord supplied the names for our
organization then known as Save Our Children. (It
has since become necessary to change the name because of a legal suit brought by the Save the Children
Federation.)

Bob understood my position and was with me all the
way, but that's not how it came across to me. Imagine
the tension at home as sponsors began to telephone
Bob and ask him what was going on, and as bookings
began to cancel because I had become too controversial!
Bob had to handle all that flack, and, boy, was it
rough. Meanwhile he saw me as getting more and more
vocal and bold, issuing potentially inflammatory public
statements, getting into areas of opinion bound to an-
tagonize numbers of our sponsors or fans.
"Don't get into the ERA hassle," he pleaded. "You're
simply not informed. The last thing you need to do is

pop off without knowing what you're saying."

"If anything I'm pro ERA at this time," I told him. "If anyone should be interested in women's rights, I should. But I intend to become thoroughly knowledge-able about the Equal Rights Amendment—and I may take a stand on that too."

So I saw Bob as both hot and cold. One day it seemed he'd be for me—very supportive—and the next day he'd seem very negative. Emotions built up within both of us to the point where an explosion had to hap-pen.

The funniest thing set it off. After praying without ceasing, I told Bob I thought we'd have to reschedule our family ski vacation to Sun Valley. Well, he blew sky high.

He raged and stormed, called me selfish, asked me how I dared to take that vacation away from the family—the whole bit. We were both so upset—each calling the other selfish, and meaning it—that we al-most came unglued.

I was at the end of my string. The Bible says, "If God be for me, who can be against me?" I felt if Bob were against me, who could be for me?

So I went to Brother Bill. Thank God for a God-fearing pastor who will minister to you in love, who will show you where you are right or wrong according to God's Word, not just human judgment.

Brother Bill showed me what Bob was feeling, his protective role as head of the family, and all that. He understood it's very hard for a woman when she's wondering if she's going to listen to God or her hus-band, when they seem to be at variance.

So through Brother Bill Chapman, God showed me to submit myself unto my husband as unto the Lord, and God would deal with Bob. Brother Bill felt, as I did, that God had called me to this purpose, but we both knew I could not go out ahead of God. Bob and I needed to be in total agreement. "Get out of this thing, if it's hurting your family, Anita," Brother Bill urged me. "You won't be letting God down. He will understand."

I felt defeated, totally whipped. I felt pulled in two opposite directions, and I didn't want to fail Bob and the family—or God. I dragged myself out of Brother Bill's office and home to the fray.

Ultimately I submitted to Bob. I told him he would make all final decisions for the family, not I, that I don't even want that responsibility. I told him I was not trying to run out ahead of him, but that I was terrified that God was speaking to me and I was immobilized when I full well knew I was hearing from the Lord.

Bob did take over the final decision making—all of it. He canceled the Sun Valley trip, even at the risk of losing a big monetary deposit. He wasn't happy about that, but he did it—and it was during the week we would have been at Sun Valley that the Lord allowed us to take part in our church's revival. (We not only got the deposit back, but through the generosity of Mr. and Mrs. Frank Hardy we were able to enjoy a long-overdue vacation with our family in the summer at the Hardys' condominium in Sun Valley, Idaho.)

Praise God! That began our family turnaround, spiritually. Bob also counseled with our pastor, worked through his own problems, and returned to support me, support the kids, handle tons of pressing business problems, and also organize the local office of the organization then known as Save Our Children, Incorporated.

Bob became a phenomenal tower of strength. He taught me, who always had been super independent, to lean on him both physically and spiritually, not to mention emotionally, during those indescribable days just past. Satan would have divided us, but God strengthened Bob and me more than ever before!

"Is *Your* Family Emotionally Healthy and Happy?" An excellent article in *Family Circle* magazine, February, 1977, stopped me with that question. It offered data based on a thought-provoking report issued by the Timberlawn Psychiatric Research Foundation in Dallas, Texas. Some of the highlights of the report are so confirmed by God's Holy Scriptures that I'm eager for you to consider them. Do read the article based on a study of forty-four volunteer families over a three-year period. Then answer the questionnaire as regards to your own family. You may be surprised at the results and take a new look at how your family makes decisions; your family's closeness; how you communicate with each other; how your family reacts when something goes wrong; your general family mood; problems you haven't been able to resolve; your family's reaction to radical changes such as death, children growing up and leaving home.

There are many things a family *can* do to strengthen the emotional health of both the individuals involved and the unit as a whole, if we will. We were interested to read what famed Christian psychiatrist Dr. O. Quentin Hyder wrote in his book *The People You Live With* in the section "The Family Altar."

This is the tradition which makes a Christian home significantly different from one in which Christ is not honored. The theocratic hierarchy is clearly taught in Scripture: Christ is the Lord of the home, the husband and father the human spiritual leader under Christ, the wife and children in subjection and obedience to him in that order. In our generation, subjection and obedience do not mean inferior status and servitude. The meaning is that it is the Christian duty of the father of the family to take on the spiritual leadership in the home . . . The ideal Christian home is one in which all members love and serve Christ as their own Lord. Where Christian love and worship of the Lord are dominant features in the home, the marriage between parents is joyful, peaceful and mutually satisfying, and the children are nurtured in security and love. Family prayers with Bible reading is the central act of worship. The whole Scripture should be studied systematically and repeatedly over the years so that the Word of God soaks permanently into the minds and hearts of all members of the family. Parents should teach their children how to come to know Christ personally. They should pray *for* their children and *with* their children, mentioning each one individually by name. Children should be taught to intercede for each other, for their parents, family, and friends and to make supplication for their own needs in conformity with God's will for their lives. Repentance, praise and giving of thanks for all things prevent self-centeredness in their prayers.

Bob and I believe that a family prayer altar provides a tremendous place of healing for emotional hurts, doubts, fears, and the like.

Years ago, when Bobby was terrified by storms, he turned that fear over to the Lord—and by faith accepted that Jesus took the fear away!

Barbara prayed for God to deliver her from nightmares and from sucking a pacifier, and He did. We'll never forget that three-year-old baby deciding to give up her pacifier—and throwing it into the bay, entirely on her own initiative, as led of the Lord.

At prayer we often discover what's troubling a child, where he or she feels sad or discouraged, or when that child needs a special little boost. As they tell God their needs, parents and brothers and sisters can move in with the kind of supportive love that tells them that their family cares—and so does God.

Dr. James Dobson, a child psychologist, says in *Hide or Seek:*

> I believe *the* most valuable contribution a parent can make to his child is to instill in him a genuine faith in God. What greater ego satisfaction could there be than knowing that the Creator of the Universe is acquainted with me, personally? That He values me more than the possession of the entire world; that He understands my fears and my anxieties . . . What a beautiful philosophy with which to "clothe" your tender child. What a fantastic message of hope and encouragement for the broken teenager who has been crushed by life's circumstances.

God constantly teaches me more about the power of love—pure, unseeking love as described in the thirteenth chapter of First Corinthians. Some time ago I decided to take each child aside at least one time a day and tell him or her that I love him. You might think it would get somewhat routine, but it doesn't. Even a big, gawky teenage boy can still put up with a big hug and kiss, even if he does protest a little—and then you decide you're glad you insisted, since it turns out he needs it even more than the others.

Bob and I also encourage our children to articulate their feelings. Sometimes we wish they'd do it less often and less loudly, but I guess we're glad all four feel the freedom to tell us what's going on inside them.

It's important to try never to condemn anyone—but especially a child. We often find it necessary to reprimand a child—sometimes quite sharply—but we guard against ever allowing him to feel that he is worthless. Indeed, they all know better than that. They're well aware that Jesus paid the ultimate price for them, and that they're precious in God's sight. We believe our kids, for the most part, know how to hate the sin but love the sinner.

Bob knows our children thrive from seeing him love me and support me and vice versa. This provides them with a security that can't be measured. Bob often includes the kids in little conspiracies on my behalf—and sometimes big ones. Once he bought a bus in my honor, a gift for our church bus ministry. It took months to put that deal over, and none of the children gave the plot away. That was Mommie's birthday surprise that year. It thrilled me so much I cried all day.

The kids still remember the excitement of keeping a secret so well and surprising me out of my mind.

We want our children to know the important place they occupy in our lives. We make a big deal of going as a family to see Bobby and Gloria run in track competition, attend Barbara's ballet recital or see how Billy's oil painting looks in the art show. They seem to enjoy one another's accomplishments.

We need to look for ways to strengthen one another and, as the Bible says, to "bear one another's burdens." A family should become a miniature church, with love and ministry the order of each day.

And finally, since God is not the author of confusion, we're trying to live one hundred percent by Ephesians 4:31, 32:

> Let all bitterness, and wrath, and anger, and clamour, and evil speaking, be put away from you, with all malice:
>
> And be ye kind one to another, tenderhearted, forgiving one another, even as God for Christ's sake hath forgiven you.

Impossible? Sometimes it seems that way. But for the Christian family, no matter how much clamor or confusion or chaos might develop suddenly on any given day, we have this comforting Scripture:

> Therefore if any man be in Christ, he is a new creature: old things are passed away. . . .
> 2 Corinthians 5:17

The Christian home should welcome change. We know we need the wind of the Holy Spirit to sweep through our dwelling and change all who live inside.

We also need periodic checkups—mind, body, and spirit. Ask God to reconstruct your family's emotions. He'll provide supernatural emotional healings for the family who seeks Him.

Anita

6

Healthy and Holy

It seems very obvious that we must be healthy if we're to become holy, but I'm constantly surprised at how few Christians really get hold of that.

I'm going to speak bluntly: God holds us parents responsible for our family's physical health, yet you can look around any church and see how many of us Christians are dropping the ball. Notice the overweight, the poor posture, the yawning and slumping, and other symptoms of fatigue.

It's not easy, but somehow we've got to get it across to parents and children that God holds each of us responsible for good stewardship where our bodies are concerned.

He formed us as a trinity—mind, body, and spirit. Sometimes you find a marvelous mind and a rare spirit in a really gross body. Now what kind of Christian witness is that?

Are your children overweight? If not, super.

But are you? If so, the well-built kids you're so proud of are very likely to follow your example. Statistics show that children of overweight parents usually follow suit when they arrive at adulthood.

All this is basic stuff—and as such, amazingly much overlooked. A healthy child tends to be active, cheerful, and competent—all of which reinforces his good health. He tends to achieve, which increases his self-image and gives him a good concept of his potential.

Every kid would like to get away with murder where eating and sleeping habits are concerned. Ours are no exception. Sometimes it takes a swat across the rear to make them know we mean business—that mealtimes and bedtimes are almost never negotiable.

Right in the middle of our strenuous winter, our household helper got hurt in an automobile accident and had to resign. Oh, how Satan must have chuckled over that! We really loved and needed Gladys, especially with this big house to take care of.

At that point, the kids pitched in. For years we've trained them to do household tasks, take responsibility for their own health and grooming, doing their homework, practicing piano, taking care of their pets, and so on. This is to the tune of "It's her turn, I did it last time"; or "I'll do it later, Mommie"; or "Why do I always have to do everything?"—I'm sure you've heard all those too!

Imagine our pleasure (almost amounting to disbelief), when our kids took over many of the household chores, including the vacuuming and sometimes cooking, without complaint, and often without anyone's assigning them a job.

Gloria, who enjoys domestic duties, began learning to cook before she could reach the range. She cleans up after herself, puts all ingredients away, and serves her masterpieces with great pride. Nowadays she's not only doing "fun cooking," though, but sticking a roast in the oven at the proper time, remembering to bake some potatoes, and instructing Barbara to set the table and make a salad while she prepares vegetables.

This has been a lifesaver. Sure we've sent out for food quite a bit during the crisis, but the girls have done more than their share of making things hum around here. And so have the boys: they're expected to make beds, clear the table, or run the vacuum cleaner, and they do.

My point is this: I can remember vividly so many days when I felt too tired to stay in behind them when they were young. Bob never has encouraged me to have nursemaids, however, even despite my often rugged schedule. He wants these kids trained—trained thoroughly—so they can stand alone when they're grown.

"They're not to assume they'll grow up and always enjoy our present standard of living, Anita," he said. "God gave us material blessings, but who's to say we'll always have them? We don't want to bring up children who expect to be waited on hand and foot, kids who are lazy or unable to take care of themselves."

He sticks to that, too. Bob is even better than I am about keeping in behind them when they're supposed to do something. Also, he's quick to praise them for a job well done. If one of the girls cooks a particular dish, he tells her it's really good and he's proud of her.

More and more I hear that modern kids aren't learning to keep house. With so many working mothers, or affluent mothers, there seems to be little time or reason to insist that girls—or boys—learn to do jobs they claim to "hate." Even Christian parents seem to fall into a syndrome of doting on their children, doing for them even at the expense of themselves, providing them with endless entertainment, rich foods, and good times.

Some Americans verge on idolatry where their kids are concerned. Nowhere else in the world is this true to the extent it is in America, but here's another odd fact that parallels it: most of our dogs and cats are overweight, too!

Are pampered children happy children?

Psychologists tend to say *no*. Pampered children often become deeply depressed because they can't find any real reason for being. They don't feel loved so much as smothered.

But what if God convicts us that our kids really aren't as lean, trim, and productive as they might be? What if we realize we're to blame—and that somehow we've acquired some overprotected, underachieving little people who, according to God's teachings, don't measure up?

It's at this point that many parents who have come under God's teaching suddenly switch the rules on their kids and turn the whole household upside down. Suddenly that little fatty has to lose twenty pounds— because mother says so. Or all snacking and television privileges get thrown out the window. The kids say they hate the parents, the home gets thrown into turmoil, and the parents end up claiming God's ways don't work in our modern world, and they'd rather return to the old habits their family was used to.

This always presents a temptation, especially in the

home where kids really do make all the decisions.

The answer? God always takes us one step at a time when He enacts changes in our lives. He begins a process within us, lets us make first one change, then another. He doesn't try to do everything at once.

The family with overweight problems could begin there. It's important to train our children to choose the proper foods in the proper amounts, and to learn to eat a variety of wholesome foods. The more matter-of-fact you make this kind of training, the easier it is to accept—even with stubborn personalities. I have some strong-willed children, but they almost always yield to quiet, firm, no-nonsense instruction.

After the diet program becomes easier to handle and the family begins to take it for granted, you might want to begin family exercise for fun and good health. There are any number of ways to accomplish this. You might want to buy family membership in a health club or your local YMCA. You might prefer jogging in your neighborhood, running at a nearby school track after dinner, or swimming a certain number of laps per day at the neighborhood pool. Or maybe it would be fun to buy bikes for each member of the family.

Unless you try it, you'll never know the benefits of family physical fitness programs. Not only does regular exercise benefit our body, it also quickens the mind and stabilizes the emotions. Beyond that, you immediately notice a big increase in interest of one family member to another, a spirit of encouragement and helpfulness, a tendency to boost one another as the whole family improves at sports. We testified to all these benefits, plus more, in our book entitled *Running the Good Race.*

Does your family have enough fun together? That's part of what it's all about, isn't it? Or does one person always end up doing most of the work—or planning—or persuading—or coercing?

Lucy Pat Curl, wife of the Rev. Bill Curl, who pastors the First Baptist Church of Orlando, Florida, wrote a challenging article in *Home Life* magazine (September, 1976) describing their methods for providing time to relate to each of their four children individually.

First, and this is so significant, Lucy Curl makes a point of saying that she and Bill make sure they get away for time together alone.

During a drive on one such occasion, as she and Bill talked about their children, he shared something he had been doing each day at the office during his private prayer time.

"Part of his desk-top decoration is a photo cube displaying individual snapshots of our four children," Lucy wrote. "He had begun the practice of rotating the cube a quarter-turn each day and praying during the day especially for the child facing him. Both of us had become increasingly aware of how easy it was to become so involved in our group that we forgot to treat each child as a separate personality. So this prayer time had become a beautiful way for him to relate to each child."

The Curls decided to go a step further: *Why not let everyone share in focusing on one family member each day?* Accordingly, each family member chose a day of the week which would be his special day: Sunday, of course, is God's Day.

They've kept the project going for six years now. Lucy Curl says the plan saves a lot of arguments. "Who gets to lick the pan of leftover batter when Mom is making a cake? Let's see, it's Tuesday, so Carol gets that privilege. A package comes in the mail addressed to THE LITTLE CURLS. No fight on hand: it's Wednesday, so it must be Scotty's job."

Do these homely ideas really work in our sophisticated age? I remember a recent article in *The Plain Truth* entitled; "Our Family Life Stinks!"

"The watchwords of the American home used to be terms such as *permanence, stability, security,*" the writer stated. "Father was the head of the home, the breadwinner, the wage earner. Mother was at home caring for the children and managing the house—and happy and proud of her role."

Today, of course, we're living in perilous times. Today is different. But Bob and I believe we'd better try some different child-rearing tactics than those used in the generation past.

Simplistic? Perhaps. Old fashioned? Definitely. But let's see now, what our more enlightened, modern and sophisticated techniques are yielding:

• "Preschoolers often grow up without the vital parental contact, guidance and example so critical in those early formative years," the article continues. "School-aged children, returning to an empty house after school, are left to their own devices. The result is sometimes shocking.

• "The Los Angeles *Times* recently reported that an estimated 30,000 children—primarily boys, ages 6 to

17—in the Los Angeles area are being sexually abused by thousands of 'gay' perverts with which the city teems.

"An investigation by the Los Angeles Police Department revealed that in nearly every instance, victimized kids came from a broken or neglected home, a home in which no strong father figure was present, or a home where mom was at work, or where the parents had abandoned their parental responsibilities. Many of these youngsters, the report showed, are simply starved for a little affection. And so they fell easy prey to the seduction of homosexual deviates who ply the streets of L.A. looking for some sexual titillation while offering 'love' to their victims." The article also points out:

• Other children, similarly neglected, turn to juvenile crime, which is on the upswing nationwide.
• Illegitimacy also increases numerically. The article goes on to report that "nationwide over 13 percent of all children are born to unmarried women, who—in 50 percent of the cases—are still teenagers. Nearly one million teenagers become pregnant every year!"

Holiness and health? The Bible says, and history confirms, that both begin at home, at mother's knee. Unfortunately, too few mothers seem to know that—or care enough if they do know.

The question is, how will Bobby and Gloria, Billy and Barbara, raise our grandchildren? Will they know how to feed their kid's minds, bodies, and spirits? Will they have enough character to rear children with good character? Will they be able to impart God's truth to their children—not just in their lips, but through their victorious lives?

The Bible says the sins of the fathers will be visited upon future generations, and this is true. And in the very last verse in the Old Testament (Malachi 4:6), it says, "And he shall turn the heart of the fathers to the children, and the heart of the children to their fathers, lest I come and smite the earth with a curse." But where we produce healthy and holy sons and daughters, we can believe God for fine grandchildren.

That's why Bob and I believe God will hold us accountable for any negligence, laziness, or indifference we exhibit in the area of nurturing our children.

After all, if God is not willing that any should perish, can we afford to be less diligent than He? As Jesus said, "Suffer little children to come unto me, and forbid them not: for of such is the kingdom of God" (Luke 18:16) Am I really assuming enough responsibility toward the little citizens of His Kingdom?

Are my children healthy enough and holy enough to please my Lord?

The Greens plant a palm tree on a lovely little island in Biscayne Bay. (Photograph by Pelham & Williamson, Miami, Florida)

This island is one of our favorite family picnic spots. Are Bob
and Gloria looking for buried treasure? (Photograph by Pelham
& Williamson, Miami, Florida)

Sundays find the Green Family at Northwest Baptist Church where I sing one of my favorite hymns, backed up by the choir. (This photograph and subsequent photos by Pelham & Williamson.) PEOPLE WEEKLY © TIME INC. *Below:* Bob and I with my Sunday-school class in a prayer circle.

Bob and I chat with our pastor, Brother Bill Chapman, outside the bus Bob gave in my name to the church. We're all on our way to a Christmas party at Villa Verde. *Below:* Bob photographs the guests, my Sunday-school class, at the party.

"Hmmm, good!" Bob seems to be saying as he samples the spaghetti.

It's Bob against the rest of us on the tennis court.

These two pictures prove that occasionally our family does get dressed up! (Even though Barbara doesn't seem too thrilled about it.) We pose for a family portrait before going out. *Below:* Bob fixes Billy's tie as we wait for the party to begin.

The crew to film the commercial for the Florida Citrus Commission gathers in the kitchen on the set. That's our good friend and Florida Citrus representative, John Baldwin, between Bob and me.

7

A Christian Father's Stand

The state of America's families—and what to do about them—became one of the major issues in last year's presidential campaigns.

The fact is, American leaders are worried about our national family life, and critics are blaming home—not society at large—as the source of trouble-prone kids. I believe that is right: I believe God will hold that individual parent responsible for his children's training, and not society.

As I dictate these thoughts, I'm looking at a desk full of clippings about family life. Not one of these stories zeroes in on the father as head of the house and responsible to God and society. No way.

In a day when parental power and authority is being constantly eroded, where is the man of the house? Our divorce rates are very high, sure, but there still are plenty of homes with fathers. In a day when there are three divorces for every five marriages, when one out of every six kids is living with only one or neither parent, where are the male voices?

Think about where you go to church. Do the women outnumber the men? In many churches today the females wield far more influence than the males, and the strong male leadership declines year by year.

We've come almost to the end of the line. If America is to turn around, if families are to be retrieved, God must raise up some men. There's a decline in church-going, yet paradoxically there's a stronger influence on national life as America begins to experience revival, and laymen from every denomination begin to commit their lives to Christ. We really live in a fast-changing world.

As I see it, the strong Christian man can have an extremely valuable place in today's society. I believe he will have an impact on America today as never before in our history.

Meanwhile, as the parents' roles diminish in every way—as we become steadily less powerful in our say-so regarding our children's education, environment, and training—there's still plenty we can do.

A clipping from the Chicago *Sun-Times* News Service quotes Dr. Kenneth Keniston's views on parental roles in education. Dr. Keniston is the first Andrew W. Mellon Professor of Human Development in the School of Humanities and Social Science at Massachusetts Institute of Technology, and holds distinguished credentials in the field of child development.

"Parents today remind me of a conductor trying to lead an orchestra when all the musicians are sitting with their backs to him and everyone is playing from different scores. Most of them are, I think, relatively helpless and confused. Increasingly they have the feeling that they are not in control."

Doctor Keniston believes that there should be a real

display of parent power over the institutions that play such an important role in family life. He also believes parents are still by far the best advocates for their children, in most cases.

Who raises our children for us?

While Dr. Keniston would not say that great corporations bring up today's children, there is some truth to it, he said. Children's physical, mental, and emotional growth are greatly influenced by business, government and schools with little or no regard for parental wishes.

On the average, children from ages four to twenty are in school—which means sixteen years of outside pressures from teachers and peers.

Doctor Keniston was quoted as mentioning the difficulty of dealing with sugar-coated cereals, and professionals in health care, inventories in supermarkets, and lack of adequate provisions for children in housing plans.

Television is typical, he says. "How many parents really want a built-in baby sitter? But what can they do?" If they refuse to have a television set in the house their children will just go to the neighbor's to watch.

Solutions are not easy, Dr. Keniston says, but they are possible. "Parents still have a role, but it is a different role than it was two hundred years ago. They should be co-ordinators and facilitators with a voice in these institutions and forces that are sharing in our child rearing. The answer comes out as a parent power, real parental control through involvement, participation, and pressure.

"These things are hard to do, but we shouldn't give up on them."

Amen! It's good to take a look at your household once in a while and make sure the priorities are squared away. A lot of men today, I suggest, refuse to get up off their apathy. They leave the children to their wives, and they don't know what's going on.

I have such high hopes for our country these days because President Carter openly calls himself a Christian. I like his stand on his faith. Too many times in the past we have had presidents who seemed to be spiritual fence-straddlers: they'd go to one church one week, another church the next week, and did not make themselves part of any church body.

The public obviously wants to have a man in office who'll say, "Hey, this is what I believe in and while I don't want to force it on you, I am a Christian and that's what I'm all about. That's what makes me tick."

I liked it when President Carter instructed staff members living together but not married either to marry or to split. I also liked it when he sent memos to his staff about giving due time to their homes and families. If he is seriously concerned about the family in America, what better place to start?

On the other side of the ledger, however, government is taking over more and more of the decision-making process as to how our children will be reared. There's the matter of public schools. There exist many Federal guidelines which affect our school systems today, and I'm sure some of them are excellent. However, take the case of Mrs. Glen Hultquist of Atlanta, whose daughter came home from high school complaining she'd just seen a sex education film that was "gross."

As the mother of six children, this Christian lady had

seen to her kids' education from every aspect. She and
her husband take a personal responsibility for knowing
each child is right with the Lord, and they have a
strong, well-functioning family. Mrs. Hultquist knew
her daughter had been informed about human repro-
duction, so she didn't understand why the girl was
upset.

She questioned her fifteen-year-old further, but the
girl was reluctant to talk. "I asked to be excused,
Mom," she told her.

"But Lisa, you're planning to go into medicine. As a
possible future doctor or nurse, surely the human body
doesn't embarrass you?"

"This isn't biology. These are moral judgments, and
they're against my religion," Lisa replied. She looked
white and angry. Hesitantly she began to describe the
film, which opened with a New Orleans stripper taking
it all off, then moved on to scenes which treated the
subjects of masturbation, venereal disease, and abortion as something positive and okay; showed ghetto
kids discussing normal and abnormal sex acts in gutter
language, and even depicted some sexual fantasies for
those who had not yet experienced any.

Other scenes showed two boys walking hand in hand
and two women clasping hands, with the script stating
such behavior represents acceptable alternate sexual
preferences. A nurse had been assigned to answer
questions from the students, and a boy objected to the
homosexual emphasis. "Don't knock it unless you've
tried it," the nurse advised him.

"But homosexuality goes against my religious beliefs. . . ." The nurse informed the kid his religious

beliefs had no place in the classroom.

Mrs. Hultquist felt sufficiently disturbed by Lisa's account of the film assigned to her school's five biology classes to phone a few people, and twenty-one concerned parents, including a minister and a member of the local school board, made an appointment to see the film. School officials cooperated fully.

"That movie was incredible!" the mother said. "I have viewed other sex education films my children saw, and approved them, but this was nothing I'd want any young person to see. The language was really filthy. It turned out that school officials had not screened it before assigning the film to those five classes. They apologized thoroughly and promised to pull that particular one from all our area schools.

"But as they told me," she went on, "we didn't think we were getting into something like this. This movie was produced by the U.S. Department of Human Resources!"

I'm saying we need to take an interest in what's going on. As society's standards lower—across the board—we can't expect the U.S. government to monitor our morals. Anyhow, the government isn't doing it.

Listen to the radio, to television, and to Citizens Band Radio, if you want some proof that the Federal Communications Commission doesn't believe in "censorship."

America's air pollution due to filthy records, TV acts, and the jokes and comments of Mr. Average Guy, as he travels across America all attest to the fact that the government keeps hands off the airways.

What's the answer? Brother Bill preached a sermon

recently where he advised us to be ". . . wise as ser-
pents and harmless as doves" (Matthew 10:16). As
Christians, we don't need to bury our heads in the
sand; just the opposite—we need to wake up and find
out how we can improve the situation.

And as we pray about these things, each Christian
man really needs to get gut-level honest with the Lord
about how far he's prepared to go for Jesus. Anita and I
got involved in this civic flap down here in Miami, and
we had to get totally honest with ourselves and the
Lord about how far we'd be willing to go for God and
decency.

It soon became obvious we'd get a lot of hassle. The
hate mail, jeers, and insults would have been a lot to
swallow right there. But the nationally organized
boycotts against your livelihood, the wires and threats
to sponsors, the demands that Anita be fired, the
threats on her life . . . .

You've just got to decide you're going all the way.
The day we decided we'd stand fast no matter what
happened—even if we lost everything we had—that
was the day God gave us a supernatural peace of mind
that never left us.

I wonder if the average person realizes we'll see more
and more persecution of Christians as time goes on.
The Bible draws a clear picture of that, and I really wish
this book could convey more about the struggle that's
taking place here as we write.

You and your home and your children will become
only as strong and as safe as you determine you will be.
You are the one who can get right with God, can train

your children in His ways, can see that your whole household is saved.

When evil arrives, it's with no warning. We didn't have time to "put on the whole armor of God." Had we not had Christ as the center of our home, we could not have withstood the assaults that have come thus far—and there may be a lot more to endure for a long, long time.

I wish I had the words to put it to you very strongly. Wake up! Take charge of your household! Make sure everybody is secure! I wish I could sit down today with every man in America and tell him what I've learned in the past six months.

But we can't even get it all in this book. We're saving the details of Anita's stand—which God expanded into a national crusade—for another book which we are writing along with this one. We've titled it *The Anita Bryant Story*.

But believe me, it's far more than just our story—it's *your* story, too.

8
A Mother's Goals

The mother whose primary goal in life is to send her children forth in maturity as outstanding citizens of the land, who is joyfully contented with the efforts of giving these children the best that she can in character training and in personal guidance will not be neurotic. Her purpose demands persistence, and her persistent efforts day by day produce joy and peace in her heart.

Mack R. Douglas said it, in his book entitled *How to Make a Habit of Succeeding.* Those words rate a big *Amen!* from me.

What kind of goals do I project for myself as a mother? Do I have a set of rigid expectations my children must live up to ? Or, on the other hand, do I play my child rearing by ear, just taking it as it comes?

I believe in goals, both for myself and for my family. I believe in taking stock periodically, just getting down with the Lord and talking straight and letting Him tell you where things need to be set right.

How in the world can anyone raise children without turning them over to God? I want to learn to see each of my kids through His eyes: He created them, and He has a perfect plan for each life. I want to be the kind of mother who can help that child work out God's plan in the early stages.

Really, it's just that simple—but it takes *time*. It takes a lot of your time and energy during the day to stop and straighten out this child or that one, or to upbuild them spiritually or emotionally. It's easy to concentrate on their food and clothes and school activities—and lose contact with the person.

Jesus said, "Seek ye first the kingdom of God, and his righteousness; and all these things shall be added unto you" (Matthew 6:33). That means seek God *first* where that child is concerned: I'm not to try to work out my own dreams or hopes or expectations through my child's life, but seek *God's* plan for his life.

I praise God for a mother who did just that for me. Mother never was a typical stage mother who was hungry to see her little girl become a star. She never pushed me, never made me practice or rehearse, never forced me to strive to meet her expectations.

Other performers weren't as fortunate as I. So many will tell you they were pushed and rushed through childhood, and when they became adults, they didn't know who they were or what they wanted from life.

My mother, like most mothers, had no special training for the job of raising children. She was still a teenager when I was born. She had little education or self-confidence, and her marriage to my dad was a rocky affair. They divorced, remarried, and divorced again, so you see she had a hard time personally and economically.

My point is this: Mother's *faith in God* helped her raise me and my younger sister, Sandra, and we knew she loved us and cared for us and accepted us as we were. Mother never tried to bend us out of shape.

Sandy, who is an extremely good dancer and was at least as talented as I, never cared to perform. I'm just the opposite: I've been a ham all my life, and really turn on when I get to sing or act or emcee.

The longer I'm involved in this motherhood business, the more I appreciate my own mother's wisdom in dealing with her two daughters. She let Sandy be Sandy and Anita be Anita, and that sums up her expectations of us. I hope I have enough sense to do the same for my four!

If I could teach my children just one thing, it would be that their primary duty in life is to seek God with all their heart and allow Him to work a work in their lives. That's it in a nutshell—the most important thing I could encourage my children to do.

It will never happen, of course, unless I'm setting some sort of godly example before them—unless *I* am right with the Lord. It has to show. They have to see you seeking God in your own life. Kids can't stand a phony adult and they can spot a phony every time.

My children know I'm not perfect, okay, but they've heard me confess my sins at the prayer altar and know it really hurts me to fail the Lord. Sometimes if I've been unfair to a kid, or lost my temper, or swatted someone who did not deserve it, I ask God to forgive me and ask that child's forgiveness also. It always amazes you to see how gracious they are, how ready to upbuild and encourage you. Sometimes they act so mature!

When a mother says she's having trouble with her children and needs help, I always say, ask yourself first if you're right with the Lord Jesus Christ in your own life. So often when you see a rebellious child you'll see his parents are even more rebellious.

A mother or father who does not know and love and obey God these days stands very little chance of success with their children. Certainly we can't depend upon society to provide much moral force—it's going downhill fast.

An article in *Redbook* magazine (April, 1977) stated that the more religious a woman is, the healthier, sexier, and happier she is.

Some sixty-five thousand women responded to *Redbook*'s survey, with 96 percent claiming they believe in God and 95 percent describing themselves as religious. Of that figure, 57 percent claimed they had become more religious in the past five years.

"A number of popular myths about religion are contradicted by our survey," the report says, including the assumption that older, less educated, and poorer people are likely to be the most religious.

An analysis of twenty-five hundred of the responses found that "the more religious a woman is, the happier she is, and that the 'very religious' women are least likely to have feelings of anxiety, tensions or worthlessness, that they suffer less from headaches or stomach upsets and are least likely to report lapses of sexual enjoyment," according to the Associated Press report of the article.

The story reports such negative symptoms were found to be most common for women who are only "slightly" religious. And the magazine concluded: "The woman who is still struggling with her doubts is the one with the headache."

When God becomes the center of a woman's life, when she deliberately places Him on the throne and kicks herself *off* the throne, she can become a real mother.

Otherwise, those children become little satellites required to orbit around *her*. She is raising *her* children, not God's children. And because *she* never had ballet lessons, she enrolls Little Cynthia at age three—and Cynthia really picks up the vibes, okay. She'd better dance, or Mommie will be unhappy—or Mommie might not love her.

On the other hand, take the mother whose life is centered in Christ, and who honestly tries to see her child through His eyes. She might consider ballet a stupid waste of time, yet she'd be willing to allow the Lord to lead her to enroll her daughter in dance classes to help her overcome awkwardness or shyness, or to build her poise and self-confidence.

It's good to encourage young boys and girls to set goals for themselves, in line with God's will for their lives. As you help that child think what he'd like to become, and some achievements he might aim toward, he begins to get excited about himself. He sees that with God, all things are possible!

We're often surprised at how realistically our children can appraise themselves and their goals. Maybe it's because they're continually making efforts in this area. This is important, because as they achieve in some new area, or manage to let the Lord help them break a bad habit or let go of a little fear, this boosts their self-confidence. Their personalities become stronger.

Doctor Leslie J. Nason, a professor at the University of Southern California, draws a vivid picture to describe a child's self-image: "You can read a child's image of himself in his actions. If he thinks he's tough, it shows. If he thinks he's afraid, it shows. If he thinks he's good, it shows. If he thinks he's bad, it shows.

"You see, he develops this image of himself in the same way we all do, by seeing how others react to what we say or do. The parent establishes the image by telling the child that he is always misbehaving or that he is a fine little boy. The teacher in school brings out the best in good students, or brings out the worst in the unruly students by continuing to comment on it time after time after time.

"But most of all we act like the person we think that we really are. It's up to us. Everyone must have some kind of a personal image to guide his behavior. It usually causes trouble only when it is wrong."

Whenever I'm tempted to think there never will be enough time to rear four children with all the care and attention God expects of me, I think of Susanna Wesley. Susanna bore nineteen children: eleven of them survived, including Charles, the renowned hymn writer, and John, the founder of Methodism.

Susanna had little money, and had to educate her children herself. By the time each baby was a year old, she had taught him to "cry softly." She set a pattern of seeing each child alone for one half hour a week to deal with his individual problems and growth, and to inspire him; and, the most poignant fact of all, she wrote that she "travailed in birth again until Christ be formed in them."

What an example! No wonder God could use such a mother to help shape two great Kingdom warriors. And since we know how Susanna started John Wesley out in life, you might appreciate this glimpse of his adult habits:

John Wesley, who traveled on horseback over land and by slow sail ship at sea, traveled a total of 250 thousand miles in his lifetime, preaching as often as fifteen times a day throughout fifty years. He had read books while making his horseback journeys, and yet, when past eighty he complained that he could not read and work more than fifteen hours a day!

The doctors told him he would have to slow down. He did—by preaching only eight times a day!

Do you believe your son could be that strong a man? I do. God always raises up great men in every generation, yet almost every great man who ever lived has credited his mother with inspiring him to rise above the average. As Dr. Leslie Weatherhead said, "God sees us as men and women in whom and through whom he can do a great work. He sees us as already serene, confident and cheerful. He sees us not as pathetic victims of life, but masters of the art of living; not wanting sympathy, but imparting help to others and therefore thinking less and less of ourselves and full, not of self-concern, but of love and laughter and a desire to serve."

I want my sons and daughters to become very successful people—successful, that is, from God's perspective. I want them to be healthy and emotionally whole, and I want their lives to be planted solidly on the rock of the Lord Jesus Christ, and their daily lives empowered by the fullness of the Holy Spirit.

By the time they leave home I hope Bobby and Gloria, Billy and Barbara will be full of wholesome attitudes. If their attitudes are right, there's nothing they can't do. *With God, all things are possible.* I want their personal attitudes to line up with God's laws.

In line with that, I hope I never am the cause of my children's selling themselves short. One of the problems in our society today is that millions of bright, well-educated young people continually underestimate themselves. Mack R. Douglas said, "Three-fourths of all the young people in America sell themselves short: they are not measuring up to their total personality, therefore they are living mediocre, meaningless existences. America can't reach her heights unless our young people are dynamically motivated to purposeful action."

Can I overdo that motivation? Am I trying to be *too* demanding and perfectionistic? I believe if you really know your child, really try to know his strengths and weaknesses, you're not likely to expect more than he really can produce.

Conversely, if you don't know that child pretty well, you're likely to be filled with unrealistic expectations of him—either way too high, or underestimating him completely.

Recently after a track meet I congratulated Gloria on placing second in a pretty close race. She really ran hard and almost came in first. "But you know, Gloria," I concluded, "you nearly won first prize. If you had been faithful in your running all summer, as you originally set out to do, you would have been first."

"Aw, Ma," Bobby said, "lay off Gloria! Second is good; she really ran good, and anyhow she almost did as good as first place . . ."

"You're right, Bobby," I told him. "I'm very happy with Gloria's running today. She really tried, and that's what counts. I *am* proud of Gloria's running—that's why I reminded her of what just a little more discipline could do."

The funny thing is, Bobby is the one who constantly urges Bob and me to expect more of him. He really wants to excel. By nature, Bobby does almost everything "as unto the Lord."

Gloria does not have Bobby's drive, but she too has high standards of excellence. I know my daughter very well. My comments did not discourage her at all. Indeed, she accepted them as an honest evaluation of the facts. There's a fine line between what encourages and discourages, what criticizes and what inspires. I don't always judge correctly, but I hope never to fail my children by expecting too little of them. God forbid!

Today is the day to begin helping our children find their own high calling in Christ Jesus. That child can begin right now—from whatever point he finds himself—to try to please Jesus.

We mothers are the channels through which God desires to pour Himself into our young. He wants their hearts and their lives. He wants us to be willing to help Him inspire that precious boy or girl to the highest point of trustworthiness and service.

Abraham Lincoln said, "Everything I am and everything I ever hope to be, I owe to my angel mother."

Napoleon said, "Let France have good mothers, and she will have good sons."

Ralph Waldo Emerson said, "Men are what their mothers made them."

And the author, John Ruskin, wrote, "My mother's influence in molding my character was conspicuous. She forced me to learn daily long chapters of the Bible by heart. To that discipline and patient, accurate resolve I owe not only much of my general power of taking pains, but the best part of my taste for literature."

Jesus loved his mother, Mary. During His final hours on earth, as He hung on the cross, He asked his disciple John to become His mother's son. The Gospels don't tell a lot about Mary's influence on Jesus, but we do know she was a meek and patient woman, willing to be taught by God.

When the angel Gabriel appeared to Mary to tell her she would bear a Son, she said, "Behold the handmaid of the Lord; be it unto me according to thy word" (Luke 1:38).

Lord, make me willing to be Your handmaid as I try to raise Your children!

9

A Strong Man's House

Or else how can one enter into a strong man's house, and spoil his goods, except he first bind the strong man? and then he will spoil his house.

Matthew 12:29

Did you ever have your house broken into? Do you ever worry that it might happen? Locks, bolts, and burglar alarm sales increase these days as more people try to protect their homes and families against the alarming numbers of burglaries, robberies, and assaults that go with stealing.

Maybe your house seems super-well protected, like ours. Maybe you think there's not much chance a nut or a criminal could get in and do damage.

Then one day you get personal threats—bomb threats maybe—and the police come over and inspect your home from top to bottom. They give you little tips about security—how this might be different or that might be slightly changed—and you get the idea the whole thing wasn't as secure as you thought. *Then you make some changes.*

Of course, before anybody could get in and spoil your goods, they'd have to bind the strong man. It's tempting to think nobody really could or would do that—that's the way men *like* to think.

I suggest tremendous numbers of America's men are being bound so silently and tightly that their houses are taken over almost without a struggle. They don't know what's going on. Thieves break in and sneak up on a man from behind—probably while he watches TV!

Of course I'm speaking figuratively: I'm not just talking about jewel and fur thieves, or those who back a truck up to your door and drive away with your stereo and five television sets. I'm talking about whoever or whatever it is that's robbing *our children* of the decent lives they're entitled to, and replacing the good values we hope to give them with worthless, dirty trash.

I'm thinking about easy sex; bad language; drugs; rebellion against authority; rejection of Christian and parental values.

I'm also talking about some of our public schools, where textbooks might make such statements as, "The story of Jesus is a myth" (from *Psychology for You*, the chapter entitled "Mythology"). Or maybe you'd prefer—if your children are to learn dirty language—at least that they not learn it from schoolbooks or so-called "educational" films.

(By the way, have you read your children's textbooks lately? If you assume they probably pretty well line up with most of the things you believe, or with normal Judeo-Christian moral standards, you might be in for a shock.)

Back in 1854, *McGuffey's Reader* published a statement that really sounds prophetic. I'll leave it to you to decide if you agree, and if it applies to our country today:

> If you can induce a community to doubt the genuineness and authenticity of the scriptures: to question the reality and obligation of religion: to hesitate, undeciding, whether there be any such thing as virtue or vice: whether there be an eternal state of retribution beyond the grave: or whether there exists any such being as God, you have broken down the barriers of moral virtue, and hoisted the flood gates of immorality and crime.
>
> I need not say, that when a people have once done this, they can no longer exist as a tranquil and happy people. Every bond that holds society together would be ruptured: fraud and treachery would take the place of confidence between man and man: the tribunals would be scenes of bribery and injustice: avarice, perjury, ambition and revenge would walk through the land, and render it more like the dwelling of savage beasts than the tranquil abode of civilized and christianized men.

I say we're getting there fast! Consider these facts:

- Planned Parenthood clinics across the nation report they're seeing more pregnant twelve-year-olds these days.
- Alcoholism is a lion prowling outside the grade-

school door, according to a coordinator of family living and drug education, who reports growing alcoholism in elementary schools.

- Violence in schools increases yearly, according to educators.
- Deliberate destruction of school property is costing every man, woman and child in America more than two dollars every year.
- Venereal disease has reached epidemic proportions nationally.
- There are more than one hundred murders per year in U.S. schools, and seventy thousand assaults on teachers.
- Students see violence as a fundamental way of life in society, according to James Harris, National Education Association president.
- Teenage abortions rose from about 191 thousand in 1972 (before the Supreme Court decision on abortion), to an estimated 325 thousand by 1975.
- Authorities estimate one-third of all abortions in the United States are obtained by teenagers.

Need I go on? The facts, the statistics make you almost physically sick. It's really bad—and getting worse by the day—as the Bible says it will. The apostle Paul wrote, "For we wrestle not against flesh and blood, but against principalities, against powers, against the rulers of the darkness of this world, against spiritual wickedness in high places" (Ephesians 6:12).

Is anybody fighting the good fight? Yes! If Anita and I learned anything at all these past five months, we've found out people will sacrifice to fight evil—once evil is exposed by the searchlight of truth. God still has plenty of good grass-roots people out there, but we need to find each other. We also need to find more Christian leaders with backbones. There's still plenty we can do!

For example, there are some five hundred parents and professional groups in America who are defending our kids against the trend toward godless humanism. According to the humanists, it's okay to teach our kids about evolution, but wrong to teach the Creation story from the Bible. You can't allow prayer in the classroom, but it's all right to explain homosexuality as an alternative life-style!

America's traditional moral stance is toppling fast in our public schools—but these groups of parents and other interested people have decided to dig in and make a fight for it.

Judi Wilson founded Concerned Christian Mothers of Opa Locka, Florida, one such organization dedicated to educating the public as to what we individuals can do about offensive subject matter that surrounds us all. I'd like to quote some good suggestions from the Concerned Christian Mothers fact sheet:

What Can I Do About Objectionable TV?

1. The moment you've seen something offensive on TV, telephone your local station. The number is in your directory. Tell them what you think. Ask for the program director.

2. Make a note of the sponsors participating in the offending program.

3. Sit down and write your local station about it, and send a copy of your note or letter to the Federal

Communications Commission. Letters are important, even if you don't receive a reply. Your station must keep them in its public file for review at license renewal time.

4. Write the sponsors. Write in care of your local station, and they will forward it, or write directly.

What Can I Do About Objectionable Radio Programming?

The above information also applies to radio programming and you may call or write your local radio stations listed in the telephone directory under their call letters.

What Can I Do About Pornography?

1. Ask theater owners, news dealers, store owners directly or by letter for cooperation in making yours a clean community. Often this will accomplish much. Express to them your grave and urgent concern as a Christian mother and woman as to their displaying of immoral and obscene material, and so forth.

2. If you see a film or material in bookstores or on newsstands that you feel may be in violation of the law, ask your police or district attorney to investigate.

3. Write to [your local newspaper] to object to offensive advertising for X-rated films, plays, articles, etc. The right of the newspaper to refuse such advertising has been clearly upheld by the law.

Write to the FCC, urging them to hold open public hearings on sex/violence on TV.

Pray daily for revival in my own life and our nation!

This excellent fact sheet also advises us, "Always write your local station to praise shows you like. Ask for more of the same!"

Concerned Christian Mothers defines its purpose this way: "To reweave the broken moral fibers of our nation by re-establishing God's preeminence in our individual and national lives. To fight the proliferation of all forms of moral and cultural pollution within our society.

The group works toward those goals by:

1. Encouraging each individual member to be involved in daily prayer seeking God's will in our daily lives and nation.

2. Education regarding God's standards.

3. Patronizing those businesses that promote decent morality.

4. Striving to promote moral values in the education of our children.

5. Encouraging the various media to promote moral programming and advertising.

6. Standing united for a healthy, moral environment for our society.

As they say, everyone talks about TV, but nobody does anything about it. That's not really true. The Rev. Donald E. Wildmon called on everyone in America who was upset with violence and fed up with sex on television to join his "Turn Off the Television Week," February 27 to March 5, 1977.

The Reverend Wildmon received enthusiastic response from more than one thousand churches across the nation. The minister's campaign came at a time when four major Protestant denominations criticized television programming. The United Methodist Church, the Church of the Brethren, and the American Lutheran Church launched a series of Television Awareness Training workshops that include results of three years of study by the three denominations.

The Southern Baptist Christian Life Commission held a series of regional public hearings on TV subject matter and content, with delegates labeling television a "clear and present danger to society." Also, the National Parent-Teacher Association completed a campaign criticizing television violence and studying the effects of television on school-age children.

Newsweek magazine (February 21, 1977) reports that children under five watch an average of 23.5 hours of television a week, compared to forty-four hours per week for adults. At that rate, today's typical teen will spend at least fifteen thousand hours of his life before the boob tube by the time he graduates from high school! That's more time than he'll spend on any other activity except sleeping.

Worse, *Newsweek* projects that "at present levels of advertising and mayhem, he will have been exposed to 350,000 commercials and vicariously participated in 18,000 murders."

How do you and your children fit into that pattern? It's not my intention to knock all television, of course. There's plenty that's entertaining and plenty that's instructive. But how much violence and trash do my kids get exposed to along the way?

Even if they're not watching objectionable material, how much time should a kid spend per week, just sitting and watching anything? Paul Kaufman, a Stanford University researcher, says, "What television basically teaches children is passivity. It creates the illusion of having been somewhere and done something and seen something, when in fact you've been sitting at home."

As I said, we don't intend to blame all the ills of society on television. The fact is, there's excellent educational value in certain shows. That's one reason the Christian radio and television networks are going to make it something tremendous. The country is ripe for family-type shows, and programs that are carefully edited by Christians in order to screen out objectionable words or phrases.

But let's wake up! Let's know what's going on in front of the small screen, what our kids are watching, and how many hours a day they spend at it. Let's think about the juvenile judges who are confronted with the fallout from some of these violent shows,when kids actually go out and commit murder in imitation of a TV plot. It has happened more than once.

A news report by Patricia McCormack states that 35 percent of never-married teenage girls fifteen to nineteen are sexually experienced. The first and most recent intercourse occurred in the girl's home—or the boy's.

"While the mother is out working or on the golf course, the nation's young lovers are finding there's no place like home," a report from the Johns Hopkins School of Hygiene and Public Health indicated. "From among the sexually active non-users of contraceptives come the unwanted pregnancies—an estimated 700,000 a year among the nation's teenagers. Social scientists call it 'an epidemic,' " wrote Miss McCormack.

It may seem strange to remind readers in a Christian book that teenagers today find their own empty houses make good trysting places. If you don't believe this information is relevant, however, I suggest you ask your pastor. He'll tell you the world has gotten too heavy even for some Christian homes to withstand. It's really sad.

When Reverend Donald Wildmon's church members surveyed a week's television viewing, they observed twenty-nine cases of implied sexual relationships—and twenty-five of those were outside marriage.

It boils down to this: Which has the greater effect on our children, the "sex education" they receive from school, talking to their peers, and watching hours and hours of television per week—or what their church, their parents, and the Word of God tells them and shows them?

Reverend Jesse L. Jackson, national president of Operation PUSH (People United to Save Humanity) wrote a mind-blowing piece on popular music for the Los Angeles *Times* syndicate. Jackson, a black, who truly concerns himself with the decadence in our society, calls the top tunes listed among the most sensitive barometers of our morals.

If you'd been watching the barometer carefully, you'd be terribly, terribly worried by now, worried for your children.

Worried because few influences reach young people as directly and as frequently as their favorite songs. Worried because the biggest hits too often prove commercial music has declared an open season on our youths' minds and morals.

Here's a handful of songs that have been hits with all kinds of listeners, including the mostly white fans of country music, soul's mostly black fans, and rock's rainbow of fans: "The Bitch is Back" by Elton John; "The Pill" by Loretta Lynn; "Ain't That a Bitch" by Johnny (Guitar) Watson; "Squeezebox" by The Who; "Love to Love You, Baby" by Donna Summer.

The Reverend Jackson says the songs sound just like the titles. "Sadly and clearly, they are syncopated pornography, musical garbage. They play on the radio and then in the heads of our children, undermining and devaluing morals and emotions . . . .

"There even are surveys that report suggestive music has led young people to—and accompanied them in—the first, and sometimes tragic, encounters with lovemaking."

Every time Anita and I write a book I suggest that parents monitor some of the records their kids are playing. Reason? The law of averages says your young men and women almost certainly have suggestive records in their collections—because the music industry knows such records sell, and consequently the market is flooded with them.

As Jesse Jackson said, "The record industry is a profitable one. Each step down the moral ladder has made more money: drug rock, sex rock, punk rock, crazy rock."

I wish all parents would listen to their kids' records—and then ask themselves what they're teaching their children, and whether it will counteract the powerful influences of "the hottest songs, sung by the hottest artists, on the scene."

Do you believe your children are not exposed to smut? I wouldn't be too sure. Smut has become a tremendous industry in the USA; it's big business, and becoming even bigger, because it's so enormously profitable.

Morality in Media, Inc., a citizens' action group in New York, says that smut ". . . appears in updated versions of the old girlie and nudist magazines; in a whole new class of paperbacks and magazines featuring sado-masochistic, homosexual and teenage sex; in a rash of so-called underground films and newspapers.

"More and more it is appearing in the content and advertising of commercially distributed movies. It has even emerged in record lyrics that portray drug usage, perversion and promiscuity as the 'in' things. And it is invading American homes through the mails in the form of unsolicited, pandering advertisements and other printed matter."

It's aimed at your family—and particularly your children and teenagers. Smut brings in more than a billion dollars annually, according to Morality in Media, and those who peddle it *aim mainly at the teenage and child market.*

Anita and I feel increasingly burdened that the vast American majority of decent parents simply *don't know* what tremendous pressures their kids are being exposed to. I suppose we might be a lot more knowledgeable than most because we keep up with the entertainment scene—that's probably where our concern springs from.

But I tell you, when a professional singer can't find decent pop songs she's willing to sing and record, it gets tough. And for the most part, that's been the case for several years now!

I give the recording industry credit for helping our nation's drug pushers, also. Rock music glorifying drugs is so commonplace, that you can't wonder that more than half of the high school seniors who graduated last spring had smoked marijuana. That figure was supplied by the National Institute on Drug Abuse in its sixth annual report to Congress.

Nearly one in every five young men between the ages of twenty and twenty-four who smokes marijuana, uses it daily, the report added. "It is clear that the use of marijuana is no longer an act of protest but a behavior that has for millions entered the mainstream of their life-styles," Dr. Robert L. DuPont, director of the Institute, told reporters.

In a book called *Sensual Drugs*, Hardin and Helen Jones ask, "What's the harm in a little marijuana?" And goes on to say that the harm is brain damage, breakage of chromosomes, loss of natural sensual-pleasure reactions, depression of sexuality, and impotence.

Do you want pot smoking legalized? Have you studied the pros and cons sufficiently to have an educated opinion?

Well, it's probably coming, ready or not. President Carter has been asked to make marijuana usage legal, on the grounds that smoking it is not an offense that should be punishable by law. Not everyone agrees with that, of course. ". . . There is increasing evidence of the steady downward diffusion of marijuana to elementary-school children. According to Peter Bensinger, head of the national Drug Enforcement Agency, the average national age of beginning marijuana is now twelve. Moreover, the fastest-growing group of drug-users are the eight to fourteen-year-olds. Present estimates indicate a majority of twelve- to thirteen-year-olds already using marijuana," states a letter to the editors of the *Atlanta Constitution*.

I'm just saying this is an issue on which the father and mother of any household should become informed. Even if I believe there's no chance *my* kids ever would be approached by pushers, I believe God also holds me responsible for protecting *all* His children. I should raise my voice in protest. I should take my head out of the sand and know what's going on.

"Therefore to him that knoweth to do good and doeth it not, to him it is sin," we're told in James 4:17. I think that says what needs saying to all us fathers who need to get up out of our television chairs and find out what's going on in our families.

How does the thief manage to bind the strong man in his own house—and then spoil his goods? I believe we families with two breadwinners can be extra vulnerable—especially if the father gets complacent.

The U.S. Labor Department says almost half of all women with children under the age of eighteen are working outside their homes, and a third of the women with pre-schoolers are in the work force according to a Newhouse News Service article. In our household, there'd be no way Anita could have her career and still have the influence she does with our kids *if I did not help her.* I'm proud of my wife, and we're both very, very grateful for our kids. But believe me, they are *our* kids, not just hers. I have diapered and rocked them, prayed with them, and spanked them almost as much as Anita has.

She has huge responsibility toward those two boys and two girls of ours—but so do I. And one thing I can give our children every day, is a strong example of support for their mother; who she is and what she stands for. That's where I think so many guys are really passive: I know I fall short, like most men, but I do know I want to be really supportive of Anita, not just for her sake and mine, but also for the kids.

On the birth of his first daughter, Lt. Commander J. P. Carr received a letter of advice from his own father:

Teach her as many of the seven hundred thousand words of the English language as you have time to, but be sure she knows that the greatest word is *GOD;* the longest word *ETERNITY;* the swiftest word *TIME;* the nearest word *NOW;* the darkest word *SIN;* the meanest word *HYPOCRISY;* and the deepest word *SOUL.*

I like that. But I also want to remember the wise words of Ruth Hampton:

> The most influential position in the nation today is held by a woman. She enforces law, practices medicine, and teaches—without degree, certificate of competence, or required training.
>
> She handles the nation's food, administers its drugs, and practices emergency first aid. This for all the spiritual, physical, and mental ills of the American family.
>
> A man literally places his life and the lives of his children in the hands of this woman—his wife.

(Both of these pieces of .wisdom are from Hands for Him, Inc., of Farmington, New Mexico.)

Ruth Hampton's words are true, and it would seem I should give my wife my total respect and cooperation, and that all men should feel this way toward the mothers of their children.

Sadly enough, however, today's hardworking wife so often really feels abandoned and alone. She sees that guy sprawled in front of TV, a beer in his hand, while she tries to handle dinner and dishes and homework and kids *after* she has worked at the office all day. It's really not fair, and it's no wonder America's marriages break up earlier and more often each year.

Brother Bill says if a guy fails in his home it doesn't matter what other kind of success he might have.

There are so many guys today, divorced and living

apart from their kids, who know that statement is true.

The forces which devastate so many homes today *can* be fought off. Not if we're indifferent, apathetic, or hopeless, of course, but only if we really do put on the whole armor of God and get busy against Satan.

I don't have to fiddle while Rome burns. There's plenty I can do! But first, a man has to ask himself how dedicated and committed he is to seeing his family be strong and succeed.

He has to commit himself to Almighty God, and then decide he's open for full-time ministry in his own home and family. As Billy Graham has said, "I believe God holds me more accountable for the souls in my household than for all the millions of other souls I might evangelize for Him."

A man knows if he's neglecting his family, and so does God. There's no use kidding ourselves.

The good news is, God always will help us turn things around, if we need to. There's still time. He could work a miracle in your home—and He will—if you first of all will give Him total control over your own life.

Trust God. Get into the Bible. Go to church, and take your family. Pray with them and for them every day. Then when Satan attacks—and he will!—your household will be armed.

I know from experience. I also know in my heart that selfish motives never have been part of my life as husband and father, and that career fame and fortune holds almost zero importance to me, especially when compared to the most important career in the world—that of being a servant before the Lord, and being the best possible husband and father.

I don't pretend to be the best father in the world, of course, but I know Who is. When I put Anita and the kids in His hands, I know He'll never let them down.

10
To God Be the Glory

Hallelujah! I praise God for the love and peace and joy in our hearts as I write the final pages of *Raising God's Children* and finish working with Bob on *The Anita Bryant Story*—the book in which we're describing our battles to maintain a decent and godly moral climate in which to rear our children and yours.

It's an incredible conflict we all are in—now a full-scale war against spreading, sprawling, firmly entrenched evil—and Bob's faith says *you* also will be one of God's foot soldiers before this year is out!

This past week has been one of total rejoicing in our household, our community, and elsewhere over the world. The *Miami Herald* headlines blazed: GAY-RIGHTS LAW IS CRUSHED; MARGIN OF VICTORY GREATER THAN 2–1; "GOD, DECENCY" IS WINNER, ANITA SAYS.

A Page One story begins:

> Dade County voters buried the gay-rights ordinance by more than 2–1 margin Tuesday after an emotional campaign-turned-crusade that had the whole nation watching.
>
> "Today the laws of God and the cultural values

of man have been vindicated," proclaimed singer Anita Bryant in a victory appearance with her husband and other leaders of Save Our Children, the group that forced the issue on the ballot and into the national spotlight with a petition drive launched in Dade's churches.

Almost 45 percent of Dade's voters, who underwent a blitz of advertising from both pro- and anti-repeal forces for the last two weeks, turned out, voting 69.3 percent for repeal—a lopsided margin that surprised both sides.

The final vote was 202,319 for repeal and 89,562 against . . .

(I must point out that "gay rights" is a media term. The issue was never "gay rights." The militant homosexuals themselves admitted that the issue was not housing or employment but that they wanted to tell us where they were at. We're not against anyone's rights, but we object, however, to flaunting what we in our religion consider sin before impressionable children— especially in the classroom whether in public, private, or religious schools, as they wanted to do in our community.)

Today, though, it's time to give God the glory. I praise Him for this book, and the circumstances in which He has given it. Bob and I can't tell anyone how to be a good parent, but God can. If any man or woman anywhere should read this book and decide to begin raising those children as unto the Lord, well, praise God, that's what we're praying for.

We just want to point others to the one Book that can

teach us how to raise those precious boys and girls He gave us—the Holy Bible.

It's a book that can't fail you: it's also the most up-to-date book of parental advice you can find. After all, the Bible tells us "God's word will never return to Him void" (see Isaiah 55:11), and it describes our Lord Jesus Christ as "the same yesterday, and to day and for ever" (Hebrews 13:8).

But you've got to immerse yourselves in the Scriptures, if they're to have a life-changing effect on your home and family. Read them daily. Read them aloud. Read them!

Bob and I warn you not to be lukewarm about your Bible. After all, any verse you don't know is a word from God that you don't possess. How many of His blessings can I afford to pass up?

For example, I remember the night I prepared to rebut the issue of homosexuality. I knew God termed it sin, but I could not quote Scripture to that effect. In fact, it took me some time to research those Scriptures—and what I discovered rebuked me. You see, since I didn't know the Scriptures which described God's attitudes toward the sin of homosexuality, I did not fully realize how tremendously grievous and offensive it is to God.

Only after I read my Bible more thoroughly did I realize my own middle-of-the-road tolerance toward sexual deviates did not square with God's view of the situation.

Dear friend, Bob and I really pray that each one of us will become more and more convicted of our ignorance of God's holy desires for us. As it says in Hosea 4:6,

> My people are destroyed for lack of knowl-
> edge: because thou hast rejected knowledge, I
> will also reject thee, that thou shalt be no priest
> to me: seeing thou hast forgotten the law of thy
> God, I will also forget my children.

Praise God for Bob Green, the strong head of our
family, who suddenly emerged as a man totally sold out
to Jesus—so much so that he's really willing to give up
everything, if necessary, so we can follow Him.

I guess most Christian wives wonder how far their
husbands will actually go for the cause of Christ—how
much He really does mean to them. Well, I thank God
that now He has answered that question for me. I remember those days when I would almost demand that
Bob become the spiritual head of our family, and he'd
say he wasn't ready—that I had known the Lord for
years, while he was a brand-new babe in Christ. That
made me so disgusted.

But God is faithful. He worked a work within Bob,
and God's timetable is perfect. Even when Anita got
impatient, God was on the ball!

Thank God for Bobby, Gloria, Billy, and Barbara
Green, too. Their daddy and mommie can tell that our
family really does have the backbone when times get
rough!

We lost bookings at times and turned down others in
order to work grueling hours for the organization opposed to the amendment in Dade County. Bob and I
took turns—he one night, I the next—tucking the kids
in at bedtime.

In fact, it seemed our family had to cut back pretty drastically on almost everything—money, time together, personal attention, household help, even shared prayer time. The kids were super aware of it all. They've shown what they're really made of, which is gratifying.

Sometimes, looking back at the challenge, I shiver at the thought of what we walked into. We did not realize our opposition would be so well organized nationally, willing to pour hundreds of thousands of dollars into the fight to obtain special privileges for their life-style to be flaunted openly in one major American metropolis—especially as teachers in private and religious schools!

The tactics they used are a tipoff to the kind of foe we must contend with in this nation. God help us!

Nor did some of us realize at the outset the scope of the personal attacks we might be called upon to endure. The *Florida Baptist Witness,* as early as March 10, 1977, editorialized about my own circumstances:

> Singer Anita Bryant has taken on the gay crowd in Miami. Bryant, a Southern Baptist and member of Northwest Baptist Church, is speaking out against a homosexual bill of rights. She is spearheading a drive to get the Miami Metro Commission to revoke a recently passed ordinance prohibiting discrimination against homosexuals. Anita is president of an opposition group called "Save Our Children, Inc." The group believes that the gay rights ordinance should be re-

pealed because it would permit homosexuals who openly profess their homosexuality to have positions of importance where they would be able to influence children to become homosexuals.

Because of her stand, our comrade in the faith has paid a high price. The Singer Company on the basis of "extensive national publicity arising from the controversial political activities" quickly cancelled a proposed television talk show series that Miss Bryant was to host causing her a lot of anxiety. However, Singer officials, apparently because of public pressure, have now reinstated her. [At this writing we are still negotiating with Singer.] . . . . A letter from a homosexual coalition group demanded that Anita be dismissed by the Florida Citrus Commission for whom she makes commercials. And to ridicule her name, homosexual militants concocted the idea of an Anita Bryant cocktail. The drink is supposed to be composed of equal parts orange juice and bigotry.

Despite the anxiety, loss of income and harassment, she intends to continue her fight to have homosexuals "keep their perversions in the privacy of their homes." Besides the campaign in Dade County, she plans to push a national movement to kill a similar bill introduced in Congress. [There have been two other bills since then.] Her crusade is supported by Dade County residents who garnered 58,918 signatures petitioning the Commission to either repeal the ordinance or set a special referendum and let the voters decide.

Anita Bryant is adamant in saying, "I am accountable to God first. Those who do not share in my conviction may continue to blacklist my talent, but with God's help they can never blacken my name."

Hang in there, Anita. We stand with you. God's word does not compromise on homosexuality. Such perversion is a sin and contrary to God's intention and desire. Legislators should always consider God's higher laws as revealed in the Scriptures before establishing civil laws that might be contrary to His will. The desire to provide equal rights for all does not mean for the Christian that biblical standards of morality should be replaced by a permissiveness in which "anything goes." To deliberately foster laws that will permit or demand that homosexuals and other sexual deviates be allowed to infiltrate every strata of society is to out-Sodom Sodom. For the protection of society, homosexuality should be controlled. Legalizing perversion gives it a respectability and sympathy it does not deserve and imposes on society dangers of frightful prospect. The possibility of school systems being required to hire homosexuals will give most parents apoplexy.

The Old and New Testaments condemn homosexuality. Leviticus 18:22 not only nixes it, but Leviticus 20:13 demands death for those involved. In I Corinthians 6:9810 the death penalty for homosexuals is not mentioned, but Paul says they will not inherit the kingdom of God and places the gays in the same category with the immoral, idolators, adulterers, thieves, covetous, drunkards, revilers and robbers.

In Romans, Paul indicates that when God is rejected and His truth is exchanged for a lie, sexual perversion is a direct result. "Even their women exchanged natural relations for unnatural ones. In the same way the men also abandoned natural relations with women and were inflamed with lust for one another. Men committed indecent acts with other men, and received in themselves the due penalty for their perversion . . . although they knew God's righteous decrees that those who do such things deserve death, they not only continue to do these very things, but also approve of those who practice them" (Romans 1:26–27, 32 New International Version).

Is there hope for the homosexual? Paul's testimony is yes. In I Corinthians 6:11, the Apostle in speaking to some of the Corinthians who at one time were sexual perverts said, "And such were some of you: but ye are washed, but ye are sanctified, but ye are justified in the name of the Lord Jesus, and by the spirit of our God."

As always the ultimate final answer for the problem of any sin is Jesus the Savior.

Amen!

"I have set the Lord always before me: because he is my right hand, I shall not be moved" (Psalms 16:8).

Pat Boone, the singer, entertainer, and my brother in Christ, was someone I had contact with during these past few months. Pat had gone on television and publicly taken a stand against a movie that portrays Christ as a homosexual.

"I'd like to help you, Pat," I said.

"You already have helped me," he replied. I wondered what he meant. Then I realized he'd taken a stand against that movie out there in California, where homosexuality is rampant. Pat said he never realized how tough a fight it would be. He had debated a homosexual minister who twisted the Scriptures around to suit his cause. "It sounded logical, and I'm sure a lot of people could agree with his reasoning," Pat Boone told me.

Brother Bill explained to me that when we want to understand God's real meaning of a particular Scripture, it's best to go to the first mention of that subject in the Bible, and go forward from there. For example, in Genesis God tells us to multiply and replenish the earth. That indicates that God planned man-woman relationships as natural marriage.

I thank God for that new insight as to how to find God's intentions as revealed by His holy Word.

"For I reckon that the sufferings of this present time are not worthy to be compared with the glory which shall be revealed in us," wrote the apostle Paul in Romans 8:18.

In Easter Week I had to really pray about things. There was so terribly much to do I had to pray to the Lord to give me extra grace and strength: I had to determine in my mind and by my will, on my knees, that I would *not* go into my office the whole week the kids were home for Easter vacation.

It took tremendous willpower after all. It seems as though we let the *urgent* push aside the important things—only this time I didn't fall into that trap. I let Bob fight the good fight while I devoted myself to our children.

One day I took the kids to the zoo with a dear friend, Evelyn Galvin, her daughter Kelly, and granddaughter. We packed a big lunch of sandwiches and drinks and fruit and had a picnic at the beach near the zoo.

We went shopping, biking, and swimming that week, too, and Bob took the kids water skiing. We had a lot of fun together.

Our church held revival services every night during spring vacation. On Friday evening there was a spaghetti supper for the youth of the church. Bobby invited his friend Keith Alexander, Gloria invited her friend Dottie King, and Bob met us over there later with the twins.

We brought Farmor, Bob's mother, home to Villa Verde to celebrate Easter with us. All day Saturday we colored Easter eggs, and held a contest to see who could make an Easter egg with the most religious significance. The kids decorated their eggs with crosses and Scripture verses, and worked very hard.

Gloria won the prize, because she said, "Easter is not dying on the Cross, but Resurrection." She had written on her egg, HE IS RISEN.

"That's it, Gloria: that's the true Easter message," we told her.

Sunday night, Brother Eddie Evans, our music minister, asked me to sing during our services at Northwest Baptist. My heart was full anyhow, because it was Easter, and it was as if my Lord had once again come alive in my heart.

Then Brother Bill announced that I would be singing "Battle Hymn of the Republic," a hymn that has a meaning to me that I cannot express in words. I have sung that majestic number at many state occasions, including at the White House, where I received the first standing ovation in White House history. Never before, however, has anyone introduced me and introduced "Battle Hymn" as Brother Bill did that evening. He touched my heart: his eloquence made it hard for me to sing . . . .

> But I say unto you, Love your enemies, bless them that curse you, do good to them that hate you, and pray for them which despitefully use you, and persecute you.
>
> Matthew 5:44

I praise God that early in the fight, He led me to form an interdenominational prayer group that meets on Thursday mornings in our house. These prayer warriors upheld me and upheld the cause through all the ups and downs, the defeats and setbacks and victories.

Because of these prayers, I knew I was safe from any physical harm; the gals constantly asked God to send angels to put a hedge of protection around me, Bob, and the children. I never experienced fear for my life.

We kept the prayer power flowing in behalf of all that

happened in our crusade, but more importantly, we prayed for America's homosexuals—and particularly the leaders who harassed us continually—and asked God for their salvation.

"God has delivered me from much sin," I told the other women. "I know perfectly well how much He longs to set others free."

So we prayed, and I must say we prayed as faithfully as we worked. And people all over America and the world interested themselves in the Dade County, Florida, struggle, and they held us up on prayer. I know they did, because we were linked into world-wide prayer chains, and many times I felt the power of a nation's prayers.

Early in the spring, the group began to ask God to supply me with His grace when I would sing for the Legislative Wives Prayer Breakfast in Tallahassee, our state capital. Mrs. Teresa Gunter and Mrs. Nancy Smathers, wives of Florida officials, had started this prayer group and invited me to give my Christian testimony while their husbands were in session. These two influential women were much on the hearts and in the prayers of our group. You see, the Equal Rights Amendment bill would come up before our legislature shortly, and we prayed that the legislature would vote wisely. With three states left to go before ERA would have sufficient votes to be ratified and made into law, Florida's vote became terribly important.

In prayer, however, prayer warriors across Florida and the nation were convinced that the Equal Rights Amendment was not God's will for the women of America. We prayed for the Florida legislature, and we prayed they'd vote to STOP ERA.

Meanwhile, the group prayed that my testimony to the legislature wives might move them to influence their husbands to vote *against* ERA—even though President and Mrs. Carter urged them to vote *for*. (We are very disappointed in some of President Carter's actions such as his refusal to take a stand on the homosexual issue as well as his stand for ERA.)

God did an amazing thing when He put circumstances together for us at last. As it happened, I gave my Christian testimony to the legislative wives prayer breakfast the very day the legislature voted on the ERA! "What timing!" I told Bob. "What's even more amazing, some of the legislators are suggesting that I might speak against the ERA while I'm there . . ."

That was an amazing opportunity, but God didn't seem to want me to testify against ERA. When the legislators asked me to speak, I could only reply that the Lord had not led me to speak out at this time.

I felt a certain amount of chagrin, truthfully. Had I started backtracking from what I believe? Was I afraid I'd offend my loyal and long-suffering sponsors? I didn't know, since I only knew God had checked me.

In prayer, I asked God to bless the legislative wives' breakfast. My dear friend Gloria Roe Robertson had flown in to accompany me on the piano, and it went beautifully; I praised Jesus for it.

And as I trusted Jesus, two fantastic things happened. First, I learned that a girl believed Jesus after hearing my testimony that morning. What's more, a Jewish girl came to hear my testimony and became as touched as anyone else. Another Jewish girl approached an older woman there, asking, "Will you tell me all you know about Jesus Christ?"

And as we prayed and ministered and shared Jesus, He was working in the legislative halls. It was exciting for Bob and me to pray with Senator and Mrs. Alan Trask before he spoke on the Senate floor. The ERA bill came up for voting that day—and was soundly defeated. Praise God He brought about such results! Praise God we prayed so faithfully, with so many, many others who cared.

As the June 7 referendum date approached, thousands of our workers—Christians, Jews, blacks, Spanish-speaking citizens—worked long, hard hours to get out the vote. Hundreds boarded city buses with brochures to hand out to riders. Dozens more manned telephones, delivered posters and press kits, funneled supplies to personnel giving leaflets to the public.

We held dozens of meetings at Villa Verde— everything from small planning sessions to full-scale receptions for several hundred, and that's when the people of our church swung into action.

Not only did my precious friends at Northwest Baptist provide every form of refreshment and service at times like that, but they provided much of the hard-core work of our organization opposed to the amendment, then known as Save Our Children. I'm thinking particularly of Cathy Miller, Tony Gainey, Lynelle Hitchcock, Peggy Chapman, Theo Sherman and Pat Atkinson. Pat is Brother Bill's secretary, and he says she made it possible for him to range far beyond the ordinary duties of Northwest Baptist Church during the crisis.

Charlie and Fredda Walker often saw that our kids got to church on time, when there were conflicts in the family's schedules, and Jody Dunton and Susan Nay spent the night and helped our kids when Bob and I were tied up. Housekeeping, baby sitting, even body-guard service was provided by fellow church members, all offered in a spirit of selfless love.

But if I started here to name all those who made themselves available to Bob and me, I'd never finish listing them. They know who they are, and I want them to know we thank God for them, and ask Him to bless them as they have blessed us.

I praise God also that in the middle of high drama, He sends us so many little funny incidents that we remember later and laugh about. Several times when I felt between a rock and a hard place, and would be about to explode with frustration, something amusing would happen.

One Sunday afternoon I was expecting several men to arrive for an important meeting at Villa Verde, when Gloria came to me with an urgent request. She wanted to spend the afternoon with several girl friends practic-ing for cheerleading tryouts the next day at school; in fact, she was counting on it.

"I can't let you go," I told her. "I've got this meeting, and there's nobody else to drive you over there. It can't be helped, Gloria."

"But, Mommie, this is *important* to me." She looked both sad and determined, and I felt stricken with a sense of how many of my children's little affairs had

had to be shoved aside those days.

"I know, Gloria. I'm so sorry, but there's just no way."

"Well, Mommie, what if you took us and another mother brought us home. Could you do that? Please?"

"Well, okay. It's not convenient at all, but I'll do it," I told her. "But we must have an understanding that you have to leave at six o'clock to be home in time for Training Union."

You can imagine my feelings when she phoned during the meeting to tell me the other mother couldn't return as early as six. I know I exploded to some extent, or was about to, when Gloria's next question totally disarmed me.

"Mommie," she asked earnestly, "will you forgive me?"

"Of course, Gloria. You know I forgive you . . . ."

"Well, Mommie, if you can forgive me, now can you just *forget* it?"

She'd touched my funny bone, of course, so I had a good laugh, forgave and forgot, and somehow all the grave issues of the day took on a new perspective.

Another time when things got pretty tense, I had to interrupt my schedule to go watch Bobby and Gloria run a relay race. Well, out of all the kids who ran, guess whose daughter found a bird's nest with four vulnerable baby birds? And guess who took them home—and tried to feed them milk with medicine droppers?

I felt like tearing my hair over that one. "I know you want to become a veterinarian, Gloria, "I told her. "But can't you please wait until you grow up?"

As tensions mounted during those final days prior to

the referendum, blessings also increased. God provided in many miraculous ways, and we had no doubt He would supply our every need according to His riches in glory, by Christ Jesus.

But I had grown terribly, terribly tired. This fatigue seemed compounded by something I could not understand at all—the unusual fact that many of America's Christian leaders seemed strangely silent. I had expected their support for our cause, yet it had not come.

By contrast, militant homosexual leaders from all parts of the country rallied to their Miami counterparts. Money was pouring in for their advertising campaigns, and it showed. So-called "gay"-supported talent from across America mounted an ambitious television and newspaper advertising blitz designed to persuade the voter.

Our organization, by contrast, had very little money. We were not nearly as well organized or prepared to seek votes. D-day approached rapidly, and the opposition had our side at a disadvantage.

Something had to be done. It was decided that I would contact every religious leader I knew or could think of, tell them our plight, and ask them to help us both with verbal and monetary support. I dreaded this chore, but I knew it had to be done.

Oral and Evelyn Roberts prayed over the telephone and asked God to protect us. "The Lord told me He will put His protection around you, and Satan can't get through," he told me. "God is going to give you a new plan. And He will send a cloud of His Spirit over Miami . . . ."

But Brother Roberts, who I so love and respect, also

let me know he doesn't like to get into other people's battles. And other Christian leaders felt the same way; maybe they couldn't support us unless their board of directors, or their closest advisors, agreed they should.

I could understand that. Certainly I know they can't jeopardize their own ministry by jumping on some other Christian bandwagon without knowing what the ramifications might be. I understood, but it made me sick. There wasn't time to explain and persuade them about the national implications—that this battle was a barometer for the rest of the nation. We needed strong male leadership, and we needed it soon.

I continued phoning, with mixed results. Jim Bakkar of the PTL Club was one of the first to help. Eldridge Cleaver said, "I think you don't know what you're getting into." Cecil Todd of Revival Fires took out an ad, however, and sent us a check. Pat Robertson, president of Christian Broadcasting Network, sent us a large check and told me to get others to match the funds.

It was hard. I would dial the phone and pray, and hope God would touch hearts on the other end of the line. "Lord, I hate trying to raise money," I told Him. "Please touch this heart and help this person see what we're trying to do for Your Kingdom . . . ."

Sometimes it worked, sometimes not. And then came the day when something in me rebelled. I thought I could not pick up that telephone one more time.

Instead, I got down on my face before the Lord. "Dear God, where are this country's strong Christian leaders?" I prayed. "Why am I all by myself in this struggle? I want to do Your will, Father, but I'm so tired and lonely and at the end of my rope. You've got to send help!

"I'm worn-out, Father. I need a rest!

"And I feel like I can't do one more thing. Where are the men? Don't You *have* any men?"

But you don't quit. You pick up and get back to work, and that's what I did. Pretty soon that prayer had been filed somewhere in the back of my mind.

At the urging of a concerned friend, Art DeMoss, who is president of National Liberty Corporation of Valley Forge, Pennsylvania, I made one more phone call—to Rev. Jerry Falwell. He is the pastor of the Thomas Road Baptist Church which has America's largest Southern Baptist church and Sunday school. Brother Falwell also heads Liberty Baptist College and "The Old Time Gospel Hour" television show in Lynchburg, Virginia. He was behind us 100 percent and he invited me to speak at his church and appear on his television program on Mother's Day.

So we traveled to Lynchburg, and I gave a typical sort of Mother's Day testimony, and I sang. Then Dr. Falwell introduced me and preached so strongly against the sin of homosexuality that I simply couldn't believe it. He asked for an offering for our organization and received a tremendous response. We returned home much encouraged and heartened.

Art DeMoss also got in touch with two direct-mail experts, Huntsinger and Jeffers, to help us campaign—and Brother Bill flew to Lynchburg before us, to explain to Dr. Falwell the facts concerning our struggle down in Dade County, Florida, and the implications for Christians and all moral people across America. The two pastors remind me of one another in their strength and dedication to God, and it was a good meeting. Brother Bill enjoyed speaking to the Liberty Baptist College student body, and also at the Wednesday-night service at Thomas Road Baptist Church.

All this resulted in Dr. Falwell's telling me, "My good friend Jack Wyrtzen of Word of Life has agreed with me and we've cancelled bookings to come on down to Miami to stage a rally to help you folks. God told me to do this, and I'm going to do it."

He mentioned a date he had in mind, and it was just ten days away! I hardly knew what to say.

"What's the biggest place in Miami?" he was asking.

"The Orange Bowl, but you can't get that . . . ."

"The next largest then," he interrupted.

"The Miami Beach Convention Center seats fifteen thousand . . . ."

"Then book it for me."

"Jerry, I can't help you with this. Much as I want to, I can't do it. I'm up to my neck . . . ."

"Just get me the auditorium and we'll do the rest. I don't need you to do anything else at all except show up for the rally."

I didn't believe that, but it was true! They accomplished the impossible. They staged that rally in just ten days!

We went, of course. Brother Falwell had sent one of his staff, Bill Faulkner, to Miami and he had worked incredibly hard to set it up. (We didn't learn until later that when Brother Falwell arrived for the rally, he was running a temperature and was in excruciating pain from a kidney infection. Throughout the evening he told no one and not until the rally was over did he permit anyone to take him to the hospital.)

When we arrived at the Center, what a thrill! As we traveled to the auditorium there was bumper-to-bumper traffic all the way—and then Bob let out a whoop of joy. "Look at the buses," he yelled. "Did you ever see so many church buses . . . ?" And it was true. From Broward County, Dade County, Lee County, buses and automobiles streamed in from every part of Florida—and they all were headed to the auditorium!

Doctor Falwell's and Jack Wyrtzen's "God and Decency Rally" turned out to be one of the most thrilling nights of my life. The Convention Center was packed; they had to turn cars away!

Inside, I saw wall-to-wall people—all kinds of people. There were Spanish Southern Baptists, Methodists, Pentecostals, Roman Catholics—you name it—all races and creeds. Our good friend, the Reverend John Huffman, formerly of Key Biscayne and now pastor of the First Presbyterian Church of Pittsburgh, Pennsylvania, had flown in. We saw Rev. Adrian Rogers, former past-president of Southern Baptist Pastors Association and now with the Tennessee Temple Baptist Church in Memphis; Rev. Jim Kennedy, Coral Ridge Presbyterian Church in Fort Lauderdale, Florida; and other faithful leaders from elsewhere in the country.

Bob and I just stared; we couldn't believe our eyes. I, who only days earlier had told God I was fighting a battle alone, shared the platform not just with my own pastor, but with ninety other men of God!

Sheriff Frank Wanicka of Lee County, Florida and his "Cops for Christ" opened the program with an impressive song. The uniformed men who profess Jesus Christ and belief in law and order drew tremendous response from the crowd. Miami Dolphins star Mike Kolen spoke, as did Brother Bill and others, and Brother Eddie Evans from our Northwest Baptist Church was there to direct a fantastic interdenominational choir. Bob and I felt overwhelmed with emotion.

And then the sound erupted, and I felt very strange—they were giving Bob and me a standing ovation! Joy flooded into my heart with a rush, and I felt beside myself with emotion, with a longing to touch and embrace those people, God's people.

Oh God, I prayed in my heart, *Forgive me! Your people are everywhere.*

Raise them up, Lord. Form a great army. Help each one of us fight the good fight. And when this battle is won, to God be the glory!

Suddenly God filled me with strength and power. Victory would be His, and His alone, and His people would persevere. *I can do all things through Christ, which strengtheneth me* (Philippians 4:13).

That is true, as true as these words of David, which I claim for my own:

In God have I put my trust: I will not be afraid what man can do unto me.

Thy vows are upon me, O God: I will render praises unto thee.

For thou hast delivered my soul from death: wilt not thou deliver my feet from falling, that I may walk before God in the light of the living?
                                                    Psalms 56:11–13

And then, standing in the packed auditorium, God's children began to sing a victory song. As the sound swelled triumphantly, my heart leaped up.

Thank You, thank You, Father God! I feel Your presence surrounding me, I see Your holy face mirrored by this sea of shining faces, and now I know.
    Thank You that it's You who, through the ages, has been raising God's children!"